3 ˄

SACRED COWS MAKE GREAT BBQS

SACRED COWS MAKE GREAT BBQS

Turning Up the Heat on Spiritual Myths

DAVE GILPIN

Authentic

First published 2010 by Authentic Media Limited
2 Presley Way, Crownhill, Milton Keynes, MK8 0ES
www.authenticmedia.co.uk

British Library Cataloguing in Publication Data
A catalogue record for this book is available from the British Library

ISBN 978-1-86024-758-3

Cover Design by Paul Airy, Four-Nine-Zero-Design
(www.fourninezerodesign.co.uk)
Printed in Great Britain by Bell and Bain, Glasgow

Myths which are believed in tend to become true.

George Orwell[1]

Acknowledgements

Thank you to my friends and editor who have helped me adapt this book from a rant into a positive addition to the Christian literary landscape. I'm still an assassin of sacred cows, but I've since become a smiling assassin!

Contents

Foreword

Sacred Cows Make Great BBQs is one of the most refreshing books
that I have read in a long time. The word 'refreshing' suggests that
it's an easy, laid-back read but that is not the case. The dictionary
definition for 'refreshing' says 'revive or reinvigorate as through
food, drink or rest . . . to stimulate'. For me this book was not only
stimulating it also had a reviving effect.

So why did I find it so refreshing? Firstly, I believe Dave Gilpin is
highly gifted at selecting relevant material on important issues. For
instance it is essential today that we reference both the Christian
world and the church world. For too long we have confined our
thoughts to the church world with limited reference to the bigger
Kingdom picture. Secondly, he voices things that many think about
and inwardly question. He manages to challenge some pretty big
issues but does so with a generous and positive spirit. There is no
sense of cynicism or negative one-upmanship. Whenever non religious Christianity is pursued there is always a jarring effect but this
is ultimately a book that 'builds up' rather than 'tears down'. In fact
perhaps I need to buy in some BBQ sauce for certain issues that
deserve a grilling.

Perhaps the chapters on the 80:20 principle and Premier League
membership provided the most food for thought. I suppose for years
I've tried to drum up greater commitment to the cause. I've put on

three-line whips for prayer meetings. On occasions I've made personal and passionate requests for people's time only to receive a greater number of polite apologies. If Dave is right it will certainly help my blood pressure.

Some of what I have shared will only make sense to you if you read the book. So thank you Dave for giving us all permission to be 'normal'. I now highly recommend the writings of a smiling assassin.

Stuart Bell
Founder of Ground Level Network and Grapevine Celebration

Introduction

Most Christian homes have one. It's either found on a mug, a fridge magnet or in the bathroom. Can you guess what it is yet? It's a copy of 'Footprints in the Sand'. I've decided that even though it's the most popular piece of Christian literature outside of the Bible itself, it's a sacred cow and I don't like it.

So much so, I've had a go at rewriting it (I have a feeling that you will instantly recognize my distinct changes). I've called it the 'BBQd Version'.

One night I dreamed of walking along the beach with the Lord.
Many scenes from my life flashed across the sky.
In each scene I noticed footprints in the sand.
Sometimes there were two sets of footprints,
other times there were one set of footprints.
This bothered me because I noticed
that during the low periods of my life,
when I was suffering from
anguish, sorrow or defeat,
I could see only one set of footprints.
So I said to the Lord,
'You promised me, Lord,
that if I followed you,

you would walk with me always.
But I have noticed that during
the most trying periods of my life
there has only been one
set of footprints in the sand.
Why, when I needed you most,
have you not been there for me?'

The Lord replied,
'Yeah, sorry about that. I would have
loved to have picked you up and given you
huggles, but I'm kind of attempting
to make a champion out of you.
If I keep putting you on my shoulders
Like that 'Footprints in the Sand' stuff,
you'll never grow past being a child.
My aim is to make you a world-beater,
a Goliath-slayer and a real History Maker.
Get it?
So would it be alright if you stopped
complaining and took it all on the chin?'

I personally think it's much better. The original has been grazing freely in the fields of Christendom for too long. It's time, methinks, to turn up the gas and heat up the griddle!

It's about time that intimate cuddles with Jesus be gazumped by increased capacity in Jesus, and it's definitely time for the wet fish approach to our faith to be replaced by a purpose-driven attitude accompanied by the signs and wonders of bruises, bumps and blisters. I have to admit it – I am attracted to sacred cows. Once I spot one, usually when I'm seated and listening to some great preaching, I tend to make a little beeline towards it to get a better look at it. After sizing it up, I usually set the table – it's meal time!

What on earth is a sacred cow? I'm glad you asked. It's something that we all accept as universally true, yet is only actually true for a certain time and place, or true within very tight parameters. And more than that, it's protected. Whoever dares lay a finger on it (or a tong) may get their fingers burnt! It may be the variety of sacred cow that believes that a certain way of doing things is essentially holy – such as the use of hymns, length of our devotional times, or even creating a cell-based church. It may be the variety of sacred cow that believes that one truth fits all, such as 'all sickness is from the devil' and 'all you need is more faith'.

Usually, these cows are, or have been, accompanied by very big things – the great Methodist Revival brought with it the hymns of Wesley, and the seeming increase in healings across the planet have largely been accompanied by 'binding the devil'. Association, however, doesn't make anything sacred or necessarily right. If it did, we'd have a 'Spit' ministry in every church just because Jesus did it.

So why am I so attracted to sacred cows? Why can't I let them graze happily next to the healthy cows and just get on with it? I think the answer is because through being a smidgen obsessive-compulsive, and also possessing a streak of perfectionism, I've regularly tried and tested a lot of the stuff that's been batted around. Believing in prosperity, however, hasn't prevented me from living in lack (as some would have it), and believing in prayer hasn't caused me to leapfrog from success to success. I've discovered that fasting (I once fasted over a hundred days in one year) doesn't necessarily bind up the devil and, no matter how much I push it, 80 per cent of my church is still carried by only 20 per cent of the people. It's not to say that what I've heard and what's being preached is all wrong, but it is to say that when certain truths become elite and a little boastful they lose much of their original potency. When sacred cows abound, people move from the field of activity to the grandstand of passivity. Lip service replaces gritty faith and real service. And that makes me even more passionate for my BBQ Manifesto.

It's time to turn up the heat on spiritual myths that have been around for much longer than they should have been. It's time for all of us to become smiling assassins of sacred cows!

Enjoy.

Dave Gilpin

PART 1:

SACRED COWS IN THE CHRISTIAN WORLD

Not everything that counts can be counted and not everything that can be counted counts.

Albert Einstein[2]

Introduction

Every day on Christian television programming we are presented with a utopian world of faith where, with a little more believing, we can enter into a place of wealth and health that's so huge we will never again have to endure any real difficulties.

It's all backed by Scripture, yet the problem is that very few people quite believe it. They 'want to believe' and have a 'belief in belief', but that is a long way short of actual believing. And the primary reason isn't simply because people are harbouring doubt, it's because the world that is being presented doesn't really line up with both the spirit and emphasis of the New Testament.

In this section, I ask the question, 'Why are instant miracles much rarer than we'd like to believe?' If God can do anything, why doesn't he simply do more than he does? Is it just our lack of faith?

In Part 1, we look at:

The Myth of Mr and Mrs Perfect
The Myth of Instant Success
The Myth of a 'Move of God'
The Myth of the Supernatural
The Myth of More Faith
The Myth of Sincerity

It's time for all of the sacred cows to be revealed and rejected, and for the real church of power to arise. More power to you!

The Myth of Mr and Mrs Perfect

The Cult of Christian Perfectionism

If you've been around church life long enough, somewhere beyond six months or so, you'll have experienced a few bumps and bruises from people not treating you as lovingly as they should! Usually, the pain subsides and we rise to live another day. That's unless we get swallowed by the myth that such injustices should never happen, and somewhere out there is a church where people are so lovely no one ever gets hurt. If you find such a church, make sure you stay clear – it isn't real! Even if it was, it would be so obsessed by not offending people that the whole place would be full of spoilt toddlers . . . miles away from the champion warriors needed to change our dying world.

Just as Fairy dish-washing liquid has become anti-bacterial, it would appear that we have created a doctrine that has produced a sanitized form of Christianity that involves avoiding being hurt, nurturing hurts, talking about hurts, and the 'group hug' style protection of hurt people.

The word 'hurt' is an unusual word in that it is generally only found at the scene and time of injury. If a football player is hurt, it's whilst being on or near the field of play where the injury took place. When in hospital, the language changes to 'injured' or 'recovering', but never continues as 'hurt'. It is only in the church that we continue to use the word 'hurt' well after the injury takes place. And that is why you cannot heal 'hurts'. Hurt is an emotive word that has a sting attached. That sting is directed to the one or the place that did the hurting. If ever there was a place where the word 'hurt' should be used sparingly – it's in the church.

It is used liberally, however, not because people simply don't want to forgive, but often because of a Nirvana type of Christianity that some people feel is their right to live out – it's a myth of perfectionism: no bruises, no hard knocks, no immense difficulties, no rebukes, no corrections, no mistakes and no tension. On top of that, there's a subtle pressure that one should be both financially dripping and brimming with 100 per cent health, creating the holy grail of the perfectionist movement. Now, before you brand me as a grumbling cynic who has a chip on his shoulder because everyone else is blessed except for him, I do drive a very nice car (thank you, Jesus!), have been blessed with an Adonis body (as well as a good dose of healthy male deception), and love the life I'm living. I'm not bitter – honestly I'm not. I just know that there are too many sacred cows in the field and they're choking the view!

Beautiful Feet

When the Bible says 'How beautiful are the feet of those who bring good news' (Rom. 10:15) it is putting a lot of effort into being poetic. The quote in Romans was taken from Isaiah 52:7 which states, 'How beautiful on the mountains are the feet of those . . .' It doesn't matter where you stick those feet, however – put them on a cushion of black velvet or on a crush of diamonds, they're still not 'beautiful'. It's talking about feet that have walked across rugged mountains, dry valleys and craggy outcrops in order to give someone some life-changing 'good news'. It's talking about bleeding feet, bruised feet, battered feet and bloated feet – they aren't beautiful in any shape or form. But just as a new born baby is pronounced beautiful (when most newborns look a little bit like an alien), so are the bloodied feet of a carrier of good news. It's poetic, not descriptive. It's what the baby represents that's beautiful – a future life, a life of possibilities . . . It's what the feet represent that's beautiful – feet that have been prepared to walk on broken glass in order to touch a generation with the good news of Christ.

'The Old Rugged Cross'

There is a famous hymn called 'The Old Rugged Cross'. Even though the words of the hymn are powerful and contain the antidote for the curse of sin, it's easy for songs and stories from old to become a tad quaint and sentimental. 'The Old Rugged Cross' can shift from the darkened hill of Golgotha to the romantic breeziness of Mills & Boon simply through the sanitizing of our twenty-first-century culture. The cross was anything but romantic and sentimental. If Jesus had died by lethal injection, there would be a syringe on top of just about every church in the world. If he'd died by electric chair, people would be wearing little electric chairs around their necks. The cross was an implement of torture, yet, because of what it represents, it's also very beautiful. Jesus' blood is gruesome, but every drop shed upon the cross is beautiful.

It's the dichotomy of the Christian life. It's tough, treacherous, difficult, costly, abrasive and abusive, yet . . . it's beautiful. Its beauty is not in its soft feet that refuse to walk a road less travelled, but in its cracked feet that show how mighty the message must be to endure so much pain on its behalf. I suspect that heaven is full of photos of feet. Each foot tells a story of sacrifice and injury on behalf of the gospel of Christ. We shall all be rewarded according to the condition of our feet. Our feet tell our story.

In Revelation 5:6, John shares a revelation he had of Jesus: 'Then I saw a Lamb, looking as if it had been slain, standing in the centre of the throne, encircled by the four living creatures and the elders.'

It amazes me that in the midst of a place of ultimate healing and perfection, there should be a bleeding lamb, not a fluffy lamb. Charles Haddon Spurgeon once asked rhetorically, 'Why should our exalted Lord appear in his wounds in glory?' to which he answered, 'The wounds of Jesus are his glories . . .'[3] His wounds are the wounds of a champion who endured such opposition – even death on a cross. His wounds tell a story of love and sacrifice that involves everyone who has ever lived.

Our wounds are not for removing but for remembrance. By them we remember what we've been through for both the enlarging of our hearts to become like the heart of our Saviour, as well as the carrying of the gospel to a world sliding into hell.

The Feet of Authenticity

It's a paradox that when we hold in our hands the gospel to present it to the world, the first thing they do is look at our feet. Our feet are the mark of our authenticity. Clean feet show a life that hasn't travelled far. Bruised feet are feet that prove that the gospel means more than personal comfort, personal protection and personal pampering. Bleeding feet show the world that you yourself reflect and mirror the love that brought heaven to earth. A stamp of authenticity makes the difference between worthlessness and ultimate worth. We know the value of the gospel, but the world values it according to the condition of our feet.

That scar of 1989 when you were on the cross for something you didn't do carries with it the proof that you must love both God and the world a lot to have carried on regardless. That bruise that will not fade from 1995 when your best friend abandoned you when you needed them most in your time of sickness, expresses a powerful love for God in that you didn't stop loving his sheep despite having every reason to abandon them for safer pastures. That limp from 2008 when the new minister ignored your talents and your history and gave the role to someone younger and much more inexperienced, is a beautiful limp. You refused to sulk, refused to leave the church for greener fields and refused to stop shining your light to the world. It's beauty beyond description.

Every time we get hurt, turn hurt into injury, turn injury into healing and turn healing into movement, we end up being stronger, more anointed and more effective than ever before. Upon our weakness God places his strength (2 Cor. 12:9). Our injury becomes another scar of a champion.

I so believe in what I'm saying that my reworking of 'Footprints in the Sand' is more than child's play. God never leaves us but many times he refuses to carry us. That one set of footprints has looked remarkably like mine for many years, as he's been creating a man who knows God, as well as a man who is becoming like his God. 'The people who know their God shall be strong, and carry out great exploits' (Dan. 11: 32, NKJV) is a promise that needs to be experienced by more and more believers.

Out of all the quotes I have ever read, my favourite is by Theodore Roosevelt who was president of the USA from 1901 to 1909. He states:

> It is not the critic who counts,
> Nor the man who points out how the strong man stumbles,
> or where the doer of deeds could have done them better.
> The credit belongs to the man who is actually in the Arena,
> whose face is marred by dust and sweat and blood,
> who strives valiantly . . .
> who knows the great enthusiasm, the great devotions,
> who spends himself in a worthy cause,
> who at best knows in the end the triumph of high achievement,
> and who at worst, if he fails, at least fails
> while daring greatly,
> so that his place shall never be with those cold and timid souls
> who have known neither victory nor defeat.

It's time for Christians to fly in the face of the sterilized, bland form of perfectionism that exists in the ranks of our churches. Let's stop the nurturing of wounds and start healing them and then parading them. They are what make us. It's time to move on, realizing we shall be hurt many times again, growing greater because of it. The more we know God, the greater we shall be. This is our true inheritance.

The Myth of Instant Success

Living for the Moment v. Living to Create a Movement

Prosperity is an odd yet beautiful beast. It's like an animal from the Dolittle collection with two heads, both at opposite ends of its body. When someone says that it's God's will for us to prosper, it's true, yet the animal can walk in two seemingly opposite directions. Pointing in one direction is a head that directly faces a land of abundance and overflow, and in the other direction is a head that faces a desert.

It would appear that in the early stages of being a Christian, say in the first few years, a lot more 'instant' miracles take place than in the subsequent stages. The two-headed animal called prosperity appears undivided as it marches directly into green pastures and still waters. As our Christian life develops, however, God's plan isn't to simply give us what we want, but to develop in us what we need – inner character, deeper faith and a patience to wait for God's perfect time and place. He wants not only to make us recipients of the blessings of heaven, but partners in the business of bringing heaven to earth! If you're living for today without building for tomorrow, you'll miss the bigger purposes of God and resist every desert with passion.

Only in deserts does real character formation and inner cleansing take place. The prosperity of our lives flourishes when stripped of worldly reliance and attachments. The prosperity beast has a method in its madness, however, when choosing to walk away from green fields and into brown wastelands; not only can it create an inner prosperity within both the heart and mind of a believer, but it can also position us for the most outstanding of 'outer' miracles. Since faith loves impossibility, deserts never stay deserts forever. They turn into amazing forests (Isa. 41:19). For those who want more than a 'quick fix', the prosperity beast leaves us with a 'double blessing'.

Living to create a movement and be a part of a movement of the Spirit wins hands down over living for the moment when it comes to its share of Scripture. At each turn of the pages of history are Movement Makers who sacrificed living for the moment, going on to become giants in the land. That is maximized prosperity – leaving a legacy of breakthrough to the next generation.

Let's Do the Maths

Alun Davies,[4] a highly influential Australian Christian leader and friend, has encouraged me greatly on the maths of life and what it is to successfully fight a 'fruit-obsessed' culture. We want our success now, even if we have to elasticize our current state of play to make it look more successful than it really is! People who live for the moment operate completely differently from those who live to create a movement. The mathematics of Moment Makers is as follows:

$$\text{Gain} - \text{Loss} = \text{Life Achievement}$$

The gains in life minus the losses in life equal the success or failure of life. For many, the current losses and sacrifices far outweigh their current fruitfulness. Many live in a constant syndrome of failure. In a fruit-obsessed world, it leads people to invent fruitfulness with evangelistic stories, retract into isolation, or reject their real call in favour of a life of quick gain and impressive result.

The maths of Movement Makers is so different. The basis of all their decisions is:

$$Seed + Faith = Future$$

Seeds sown, plus faith to believe in things unseen, equals an amazing future. The Movement Maker's life may look like a field of brown dirt, yet underneath is the golden seed of tomorrow's world. Movement Makers may have very little to show for themselves because they give away more than they keep; but in the end they make history, rather than just ending up as a *part* of history.

There are a number of problems with being fruit-obsessed:

Firstly, you can't create fruit. In 1 Corinthians 3:6 Paul wrote: 'I planted the seed, Apollos watered it, but God made it grow.' Fruit belongs to God. You can, however, plant seed any time, any day. Moment Makers are waiting for the moment, while Movement Makers are creating history today by planting seeds in season and out.

Secondly, fruit is the evidence of yesterday. It's the result of yesterday's seed sowing. If you live for the moment you'll always be half-frozen in history. Fruit is final. Seed is the future.

Thirdly, fruit is momentary. You can't keep it. You can try to preserve it, but it can rarely be kept outside of a memory. Fruit obsession leads to frantic desperation for more fruit the moment the current fruit begins to wane. Seed obsession is never thwarted. There's always seed to sow. There's always more fruit grown by 'seed-sowers' because of the higher number of seeds actually being placed in the ground compared to those who are simply fruit-obsessed.

Hebrews 11 is one of the most interesting chapters in the Bible. We often call it the Hall of Faith or the Heroes of Heaven chapter. It is, however, a list of people who actually never really made it in their lifetimes, despite their faith. The first in line is Abel, killed by his brother. Enoch is mentioned next and he simply disappeared one day. Noah saw his friends drown. Abraham died with only one son from a promise of thousands, and only owning a small block of land from a promise of territories. Even the amazingly heroic events in the life of Isaac, Jacob and Joseph are not mentioned – only their faith in the future. The parting of the Red Sea and the walls of Jericho falling down are neither accredited to Moses or Joshua but to the people. What's going on? In a quick summary of Gideon through to Samuel, we see that 'faith conquered kingdoms', but that is only squeezed into two verses before reverting back to people who saw a seeming reversal of fortune (sawn in two for example) but believed a lot.

This chapter does not belong to people who live for the moment. Many of our heroes failed dismally in the mathematics of Moment Makers. They succeeded, however, in the maths of Movement Makers. The seed they sowed in obedience and faith had more impact after death than before it. They sowed their seed into a generational God – a God of Abraham, Isaac and Jacob . . . a God of history. They may have been unimportant in their day when it came to the nations of the world, yet they were actually the most significant people on earth. Their legacy remains today – even the blood of Abel, poured out as a beautiful act of generosity to a God he'd never seen.

The Law of Hard

Hebrews 12 begins with some of the most difficult and dismissive theology in the Bible. The essence of it is found in the simple phrase 'Endure hardship as discipline' (Heb. 12:7). It is all about the Law of Hard. When something is too hard, we often draw back. However, when someone endures hardship, is trained by it and incorporates it as a part of God's providence, they get to receive a 'harvest of righteousness and peace' (Heb. 12:11).

It's from that harvest that seeds of character are gathered and planted in the next generation. Everyone spawns seed of some variety that eventually gets picked up by the soil of the next generation. Character is a stronger seed than the Word of God alone because it is the Word outworked in our lives. It's what shapes the future. They will not do as we say, they'll do as we are. It's the heavenly harvest of character that changes us from being compromised, timid and weak followers of Christ, into fearless, generous and strong believers in Christ. And it's *through* hardship, not *despite* it. Hardship here is undefined but incorporates anything that's difficult. Many teachers who major on abundance and blessing refuse to see how a loving God can allow anyone to go through hardship and pain when God has the capacity to relieve it. It's this one-dimensional view of blessing and of God's nature that has kept the church shallow and suffocated. It's time for real History Makers to emerge carrying all the necessary seeds of character – seeds that have the power to change not just this generation, but the next.

Who's the Greatest?

In the light of living by faith, and living to create a movement, who is the greatest History Maker – Billy Graham or Edward Kimball? Billy Graham is seen as the twentieth century's greatest evangelist, seeing millions of souls won for Christ. Edward Kimball was a Sunday school teacher, responsible for only a few won for Christ.

There are 5 degrees of separation between the two of them. Billy Graham was saved at a crusade held by Mordecai Ham in his home town of Charlotte in 1934. Mordecai Ham was there at the invitation of a Christian association that arose from meetings Billy

Sunday held in the town a decade earlier. Billy Sunday worked for a period of time with J. Wilber Chapman, who had his faith affirmed by D.L. Moody, who himself saw over a million souls saved in his lifetime. D.L. Moody was saved through his Sunday school teacher – Edward Kimball.

The spirit of our age would say that Billy Graham is the greater of the two, yet the spirit of Hebrews 11 would err on the side of Edward Kimball. If faith is believing in an unseen future, Edward lived by faith. If living to create a movement is more about what you sow than what you reap, then Edward was a Movement Maker.

Charles Haddon Spurgeon was saved in the mid 1800s to become one of Britain's greatest preachers and church leaders. He was saved at 15 years of age in a primitive Methodist church attended by around fifteen people on a snowy Sunday morning. The minister was snowed in and 'a very thin looking man, a shoemaker, a tailor, or something of that sort,' went up into the pulpit to preach a life-saving message.[5] Again, who was the greatest History Maker – Spurgeon or the shoemaker? Both would be credited highly by the standards of Hebrews 11, yet if push came to shove, it would be swayed towards the shoemaker.

It's time for us to see ourselves as Movement Makers alongside the Edward Kimballs and the shoemakers of this world. This is our moment to live to create a movement that will not only see us doubly blessed, but bless the generations that follow.

The Myth of a 'Move of God'

Is It really a 'Move of God'?

Whenever someone claims that what they're currently experiencing is a 'move of God' I wonder what was happening to them before God moved! Throughout the past ten years, there have been many places across the world that have been branded as experiencing 'a move of God'. If that's the case, what does this say about what's happening in my neck of the woods? Does it mean that what I have is less than what they have? Does it mean that before 'God dropped in' there was an absence of God? I sure hope not.

I believe in the sentiment behind 'a move of God'. I want a 'move of God'. I also want to see a mass movement of people entering into the kingdom of God, blowing our expectations right out of the water! What I'm wanting, however, is not actually a 'move of God' – I'm wanting a 'move of people'. I'm looking for a *people movement.* Because God never actually stops moving, a 'move of God' is a poorly coined expression that often masks an inferiority complex that has not been dealt with, yet which most Christians are unaware of.

The only time that God's movements are ever slowed down amongst the saints is when individuals vacate the seat of faith. At all other times – he's moving. He's knocking on doors to the heart; he's leading the blind; he's protecting the weak; he's empowering the goings out and comings in of his people. He's always moving, like the wind.

It all originates from the same lack of spiritual confidence that refers to the 'manifestation of the Spirit' every time as the 'gifts' of the Spirit. In 1 Corinthians 12:7, the word 'manifestation' is used when referring to the nine 'gifts' given by the Spirit. It's our lack of confidence that often makes us think we have nothing until a gift is given. The scriptural idea presented is that we have everything – it just needs releasing from within us! 'Manifestation' presumes hidden presence. All nine 'gifts' are in essence nine manifestations of a God who resides in the heart of the born again. For a Spirit-filled church, it is much healthier to sing 'Holy Spirit rise' than 'Holy Spirit fall'. In that way, we become aware that we're still in possession of what we felt at that particular time we sensed God 'fall' a long time after the 'falling' has passed.

Inferiority Complex

The human spirit has a bias for acknowledging the God of eternity who sits in the heavens, over and above the internally residing Spirit of eternity. This bias is caused by both an inferiority complex and a 'hormone' replacement of faith with feelings. We don't feel powerful. We feel our failings and our inadequacies. It's because our human spirit searches for water beyond the river, instead of drawing from the river itself, which currently flows from its inmost being (John 7:38).

In the running of our weekend services, I am constantly reminding my ministry team to 'declare' blessing more than 'pray' for blessing. There are parts of our services where we especially connect to the needs and emotions of the congregation through perhaps a word of prophecy or a word of knowledge. One of my ministry team leading the meeting will then ask those who feel that the word is for them to lift their hands and get ready for a further impartation of the Spirit. It's at this crucial point that confidence leakage in the leader often occurs. Prayers are prayed instead of declarations declared. The same can happen for each of us – we can lose our confidence and reduce our lives to simply 'asking God' for stuff instead of prophetically declaring both his praises and his provision over our lives. Even though the Lord's Prayer is a combination of both prayer and declaration, Jesus never 'prayed' for the sick and never openly prayed for provision. He declared 'be healed' and he 'gave thanks' and he 'rebuked the spirit' but, under the influence of the Spirit, never asked his Father to do what he believed he could do through the Spirit's enablement. This baton of confidence was then carried by his disciples, one of whom famously declared, 'Silver or gold I do not have, but what I have I give you. In the name of Jesus . . . walk' (Acts 3:6). He took on the name of Jesus and touched the crippled man in the power of the Spirit. He may have lacked in finance, but he didn't lack in confidence.

Don't misunderstand me. It's good to pray. Jesus taught us to pray. To paraphrase 2 Chronicles 7:14: 'If my people pray, I'll heal their land.' It's just that much of our praying, as opposed to declaring, comes out of a lack of believing and a lack of acknowledging the real power invested in us through the Holy Spirit's residency.

In our own church, because people can easily pick up on the wavering of our confidence, our Sunday 'prayers' are often met with a quiet but respectful 'amen'. It's so different when we move into declaration. These are often met with a noisy rise of affirmation and agreement. That rise shows how the climate changes according to the confidence exuded.

Praying for the Lost

While on the subject of prayer, and just to be controversial, praying for the salvation of souls is not a prayer Jesus encouraged us to pray (even though I do it a lot!). Out of all of the things that our God can do, making someone get saved is not one of them. He never overrides a person's right to choose. What he *can* do, however, is set the culture to make it easier for a right decision to be made. God can hold back demonic clouds and lead a person to life-giving water. All they have to do then is choose. Because this process involves our participation as well as theirs, Jesus did urge us to pray that God would send out 'labourers' into the fields that are ripe for the picking.

Because 'our moving' is a large part of 'God moving', it's true to say that as long as we're moving, God's moving. People who are simply and solely 'waiting' for a move of God find themselves in a stalemate situation. God is waiting for them to move!

I'm in Revival

When starting a church plant in Leeds, I was asked by a man who'd been around church life for quite some time when I thought revival was going to come to Britain. I told him that he was looking at it. I am in revival. It's great! Maybe it's different to all it's hyped up to be, but it really is brilliant. The only times I haven't been in revival is when I've vacated the seat of faith and entered the corridor of sin and striving. At all other times – I've been in revival. Swimming in it! His perception was one of waiting for a sovereign move outside of our involvement. As long as I'm moving, God is moving. As long as God's moving, and he never ceases to move, I'm moving. My movements are proof of a God at work. Prompted by the Spirit, obeying the Spirit, and being nurtured by the Spirit – this is the revival so many are longing for. This is 'a move of God'.

To attach a 'move' to a collection of dramatic healings is to detach it from a daily collection of more subtle moving, yet just as profound. It may be true that if we prayed more diligently then God may pour out a greater array of both the subtle and the spectacular, but it cannot be said that the power taken to instantly heal a migraine is of lesser quality or quantity than that taken to heal cancer. The power needed to heal even the greatest of human diseases still lies on the fringe of his creative ability, along with his power to heal a simple headache. They're both a work of heaven.

At the start of my ministry as a youth pastor, I believed for very small amounts of money that would get my wife and me through the following week. I no longer do that. I believe for hundreds of thousands of pounds to complete our church's building projects. It's not more faith and the outcome is only greater in that the answer to my faith now involves a change of thinking of many more people in order to complete the vision. It is not a miracle of greater size. A miracle is a miracle is a miracle.

Jesus did say, however, that 'greater works [we] will do' (John 14:12, NKJV). Because his range went from winemaking to dead-raising, it is obvious that the word 'greater' doesn't mean in scope but in amount. The Holy Spirit's power would no longer be confined to one man and his disciples.

I've found that lurking within most Christians is a feeling that they simply don't deserve a move of God and that's why he's always moving elsewhere. The greatest reason for this is a religious spirit of condemnation that, when left unchecked, declares that we just don't quite make the grade. We begin to take the side of slavishness over sonship, focusing more on our weaknesses, misgivings, failures and sins rather than his blood, our strengths, our success in him and his victory in us.

The problem with religious spirits is that, in their piety, they not only create mass inferiority and a sense of failure, they can also create a strain of superiority and a sense of having made it. Missionaries are no less prone to this deception than the rest of us. In their zeal to communicate their vision and achievements to their 'home' church, they can so easily spawn the spirit of 'What are you fat, comfortable, consumerist westerners really doing for God, while the rest of the world goes to hell?' Spurred on by a growing resentment at having received such little financial and communicative support, their spiel ensures that the listeners are left feeling that it's only the missionary who's cutting it in a far-flung land. This in turn leads to even greater paralysis in the movements of the people in the 'home' church.

The Cutting Edge

All of this exposes another spiritual myth of some people being 'on the cutting edge' or 'on the front line' of Christianity, while others are not. Paddling up the Amazon looking out for unreached tribes is seen as the 'front line', while putting out the washing and saying hello to the suburban neighbours is not. As I have pointed out in my previous book, *Jesus, Save Me from Your Followers!*,[6] it often leads people to believe that the people sitting next to Jesus after we all get to heaven must be either a 'Hudson Taylor' or 'Mother Teresa' type. The truth of the kingdom is that our rewards come from what we do with what we have, and not where we do it and in what century we do it in.

In Search of Great Faith

In defence of the church in the western world, I have two things to say. Firstly, there are only two places in the Gospels where Jesus claimed that someone had 'great faith'. The first was the centurion leader regarding his paralysed servant (Matt. 8:10), and the second was the Canaanite woman who claimed that even the dogs ate the crumbs that fell from the master's table (Matt. 15:28). In both cases, Jesus was not geographically present at the place where the miracle happened. For the woman with the issue of blood, the two blind men, as well as the ten lepers, Jesus was present, not absent. Because none of us have ever seen Jesus, touched him or heard him in a tangible, physical sense, the faith we operate in is always what Jesus defined as 'great faith'. We believe each day, not only with the physical absence of Jesus but often in the complete absence of demonstrative miracles and healings. While Christians in many third-world countries may regularly see the more obvious wonders of God, we continue to believe in their absence. That is nothing other than 'great faith'.

Secondly, all of us are on the 'front line'. Our enemy is the clear gas of consumerism and selfism. It takes both the wisdom and power of God to discern it, counteract it and walk unswervingly through it. This can be a harder opposition to overcome than the more obvious opposition of persecution and hatred. To own things and not love things needs the constant cleansing by generosity, as well as a disciplined refocusing on spiritual values which may not be needed in places where there's generally an absence of 'things'.

Why Do Churches Grow and Decline?

When a church in our nation suddenly mushrooms in size, it is often claimed that they're experiencing a 'move of God'. In the general spirit of good sportsmanship, I usually comply with the comment but don't necessarily agree with it. 'Moves of God' that cause churches to suddenly rocket in size, I believe, can actually have nothing to do with the movements of God. People join churches for many reasons. For some, it's because their friends have moved there and they don't want to live life without them. For others, it's the need to be 'where it's at' or to be a part of 'the next big thing'. For others, it's because they like the minister or the music or the length of service. For others, it's because the kids love it. They're all good reasons but they may simply all be led by the human soul rather than the Spirit. Looking for belonging, identity and security are all basic needs of humanity and it's these basic needs that direct much of the movements of people from one church to the next. It's the urgings of the soul rather than the promptings of the Spirit that so often inflate one church and deflate another nearby. Jesus did meet 'felt' needs, but when the rubber hit the road, he removed the immediate benefits and held out for faith-filled discipleship. 'Moves of God' are based on a sense of call, a revelation of God's Word and a transformation of a person from the inside out.

The movement of people from one church to another can actually hinder a move of God while being classified as one. When people get 'saved', the real proof that their response is beyond the meeting of 'felt' needs is found in the profound change that takes place on the inside of their hearts, resulting in relational, attitudinal and behavioural changes. Only then can it be confirmed to be a 'move of the Spirit'.

Let's be determined to always be a part of the moving of God, and never allow our lack of confidence to rank someone else's move as more significant than ours. It's all God and it's all good!

The Myth of the Supernatural

4

Why Are Creative Miracles Still So Rare?

We all live in a miracle-obsessed Christian age. Every other generation believed in miracles, but ours *really* does! Almost every
Christian channel on the television devotes almost every hour of
transmission to promoting them. What I want to know is – do we
see loads more miracles now because we believe 'more', or is our
believing simply a 'want to believe'? Has the *real* miracle count
increased a *lot*, or just increased? Is our believing a *real* belief or is
it in essence a 'belief in belief'? I realize that I'm in dangerous territory that is often occupied by cynics and mockers, but I'm willing
to risk it in the cause of healthy thinking!

With so much fascination with miracle hot spots over the earth,
is our huge craving to see the supernatural driven by a healthy quest
for more of God, or is it being driven by an unhealthy deficiency in
our understanding of how God really works? If we struggle with
believing something, we can find ourselves always looking for proof
that that something is true. If we're unsure about the love someone
has for us, we can find ourselves looking for, and ever demanding,
proof of that love. And that applies to people's walk with God as
well. When we're not sure about the favour and presence of God, we
will always be looking for affirmative 'signs' wherever we go.

Creative miracles, where God instantly joins bone to bone or
instantly recreates a vital organ in someone's body, are still quite

rare in our country. Even when prayer is pumping and expectation is high, the number of 'creative' miracles that occur over either the short or long term remains on the low side. Many would say that it is because people just don't believe in God's ability to heal and deliver. This is attributed to the fact that Jesus himself could not perform many miracles in his home town because they refused to see him as anything else but the carpenter's son. For many, this is a real truth. But the thing about believing is that you can't actually just turn it on like a tap whenever you want God to do something special. It's not purely a decision and it's not an emotion – it's a gift that only heaven can give. Sure, a lot of people do harbour doubts and unbelief, but there are a lot of people gagging for God to speak specifically into their situation who have currently not heard directly from heaven. They've got a general word but not a specific word.

Miracles, Wonders and Signs

Because of a need to visibly see the workings of God, little room is left for the huge side of God that actually sets up many of the outstanding and significant miracles of God in the Bible – his ability to put people in all the right places, and at all the right times, as well as his ability to transform the hearts and lives of stubborn people.

In Acts 2:22, Peter claims that Jesus was 'accredited by God' through 'miracles, wonders and signs'. In describing the miraculous ministry of Jesus in three distinct categories, we can note that not every 'miracle' is a creative miracle. A wonder or a sign could very much be a non-creative miracle, such as the finding of money in the mouth of a fish, or in the provision of a donkey for Jesus to ride upon.

In a quick review of the proliferation of the miraculous in our time, it appears that non-creative miracles, which include bumping into certain people at certain times and being in the right place at the right time, outnumber creative ones 1,000–1, even in a 'faith-filled' environment.

Again, why doesn't God do more in the way of pizzazzy miracles when he has the power to do what he likes when he likes, especially when people are all-believing and all-expecting? I have personally prayed for finance hundreds of times and, even though God has provided, he has never once, to my knowledge, created a money tree outside my back door. I cannot even verify that God has actually created new banknotes or reprinted banknotes that have gone out of circulation so as to produce 'legal tender'. What he has done, though, is provided miraculously through people. It's a non creative miracle that is often dressed up as a creative one to make it seem more miraculous. A miracle is still a work of God however, whatever type it may be. The celebration needs to be just as big however it came to pass. Why, however, doesn't God simply use the power invested in him and let loose upon the earth?

One explanation for the lack of financial 'super' miracles is that they involve less of God's power that we would at first realize. The trickier miracles are the non-creative ones that include both the transforming of a human heart by making it willing to part with its cash, and the repositioning of people so as to place all the right people in all the right places at all the right times to provide the pipeline for financial transfer.

If I'm praying for £1,000, God will need to work on someone's heart in order that that money (or part of it) can be released from their pocket to my need. He has to at some stage let them know of my need or my existence and give them a reason to pass it on. All of that takes as much miraculous power as it would do to create a crisp, new banknote out of thin air.

This can also, in some way, be applied to the provision of healing. I have heard of hundreds of testimonies where, despite the mysterious absence of creative miracles, people have found themselves in the hands of a particular surgeon and placed with particular people who have made steps towards Christ. This new connection wouldn't have occurred with a slam dunk miracle. It may not be our perfect scenario, yet it is one that is played out over and over again by people of faith. They're open and eager for the stupendous miracles of God, and they're open to the vast army of mini miracles from God.

Each display of non-creative miracles (which include transformational, positional and providential miracles) is just as much a show of power as blind Bartimaeus' eyes being restored. It's just impossible for us to believe it without a faith in the invisible realms of the Holy Spirit. One of the real purposes of creative miracles has been to provide spasmodic and irregular portals into a world that neither sleeps nor slumbers (see Ps. 121:4) – a world of non-stop miracles. It's just that so many are not so obvious.

Super Size Me

For many years after starting a new church in the north of England, I was accosted by people who claimed to have received truckloads of prophecies from heaven. They received them in almost daily succession. I wondered on many occasions if I was a little backslidden because of my lack of daily – or even weekly – 'thus saith the Lords'. How did they get so many prophecies and words so often? My conclusion was that they had become a little too imaginative – not in an evil sense, or even in a conscious sense, but more in desperation in having to hear from heaven. It's another case of really 'wanting to believe' and in so doing, potentially manufacturing the evidence of God's presence and power.

Super-spiritual people who grasp for the supernatural of God tend to be people who have not grasped the very real and very comforting words of faith that God offers to them, often because of underlying hurts and disappointments. Dramatic faith stories can, at times, mask a low faith level that usually teeters on the fence between holding onto God and falling away from him altogether. When confronted by their inner discrepancies and possible hurts, many either go back into the world they once rejected or head for a new church that won't confront them on any real issues of the heart.

Not only that but our attempt, at times, to maximize the more stupendous and dramatic side of the workings of God has encouraged passages like Isaiah 53 to be dislodged from their principal purpose of rectifying the diseases of sin to rectifying the diseases of the body. The cross certainly presents us with a holistic future, yet the dislodging of the passage has kept many people still caught in the habits of sin and fear that Christ has released them from. As well as that, the direct association of sickness with the demonic is something that the New Testament rarely does. Over-enthusiasm has called everything from possessing autism to addiction to nicotine a demonic manifestation. There is one big problem with this – it's rarely true. It *is* true that the demonic is often accompanied by disability, but to claim all sickness and disease is demonic is over-egging the pudding – its residue is to create a backlash of fear and depression amongst the world you've tried to help.

The Christian Media

This over-egging of the super-miraculous has been exacerbated by the huge expansion of Christian television. In a medium that wants to both inform and entertain, the Christian broadcasters often find themselves generally swayed by an over-injection of prosperity ministries that deal primarily in the two subjects of healing and money. In doing so, they attract and create a type of Christianity that feeds off the dramatic and the unusual, creating a dissatisfaction in the viewer within the context of their own local church. The local church, however, is dealing with a set of wider spiritual spectacles which encompass patience, winning the lost, holiness and faithfulness (without taking their eyes off abundance and the creative power of God), and consequently finds it hard to compete with the sensational message and methods incorporated by many of the television evangelists and teachers.

Once you start a 'miracle' bandwagon, it's hard to stop it. It creates its own pressure to continue to sensationalize the Christian faith. This has led to a whole array of traits, including:

1. The over-egging of manifestations

There is no doubt that falling under the power is a legitimate manifestation of the Holy Spirit. A loss of balance and an 'overcoming' are experienced by many a sincere Christian. But along with the authentic manifestations – as well as the auto-suggestive manifestations (when falling becomes the thing you do) – comes the nudging of people to get them to fall. It's a silly habit by some that masks the pressure of having to look as if something is really happening, whether it is or not. Faking the effects of the Holy Spirit can have a detrimental effect upon both the minister doing it as well as the more authentic local church that can't keep up with it. (I do understand, however, that in sincerity some do push a little simply out of their passion to impart something into the person's spirit.)

2. The overplaying of special numbers

There is no doubt that numbers in the Bible signify things of importance. The number 7 signifies perfection, the number 12 signifies governmental authority, and the number 40 represents cleansing and the end of a season. The problem comes when someone gets a number planted in their head and proceeds to tell the viewer that there is an anointing on that number. It's usually associated with the act of getting people to give their money over to the ministry. Even if the specific number – such as 38 – has some limited anointing by being applicable to a very narrow situation, it is unwise to give that number out to a wider audience. It eventually creates superstition, which is what the Bible sets itself apart from; 38 becomes 'my lucky number' and I believe that God will bless me on that basis. It's a product of trying to be dramatic and drum up exciting results. It's all at variance with a New Testament culture.

3. The overstating of paraphernalia

Everyone can be made to have an unhealthy interest in angels, gold dust, gold teeth and strange behavioural patterns! It's right to observe them, but it is wrong to be sidetracked by them and to create a franchising ministry out of them. The Epistles never once talk about the 'Shadow' ministry begun by Peter. It never refers to 'Sling' ministries launched by David. Yet, each of these was a unique method used at a unique time by the creative God. They weren't franchised, only observed.

Immaturity often hankers after such things as a compensation mechanism for not knowing enough of God. The book of Hebrews is all to do with a refocusing from angelic ministry to the real ministry of Jesus. It may not get the hairs on your neck up, but it holds the key to the real knowledge of God.

4. The overemphasizing of certain doctrine

Some Christians hold an incredibly keen interest in subjects such as the nation of Israel, the second coming, the rapture, the anti-Christ, Bible prophecy and the gifts of the Spirit. In each one of those subject areas, God has raised up men and women anointed by God to herald their validity and place in Scripture, but for many their doctrine has become such an exclusive and prized one that they are permanently distracted from keeping the main thing the main thing – knowing Christ and making him known. Majoring on minors often produces an arrogance that has no place in the kingdom. The proof of maturity is that someone readily lays aside their speciality subject for the main themes of grace, salvation, growth, maturity, the church, ministry, leadership and eternity. Hebrews also lists repentance, faith, baptisms, impartation, resurrection and judgement as its foundational platform. If this is the foundational thrust of the Bible, it must be ours as well.

Recently, out of curiosity and frivolity, my teenage son rang up for some 'Miracle spring water' from a well-known television ministry. In return, he received a letter which included 'personal' prophecy and a 'personal' word of knowledge that were obviously not personal at all. It appears that God is confused about the masculine nature of my son as the prophecy began 'Fear not, my daughter'. Since that letter, he has received miracle seeds, miracle oil, miracle beads and other paraphernalia, as well as requests for huge sums of money. All of the giving was directed by 'magic' numbers and it all played into the hands of fear rather than real faith. It's obviously a time for many Christian stations to review their content in line with real New Testament truth and emphasis.

In a faith-filled culture, the rare specialness of dramatic miracles as well as the general spasmodic nature of the super-miracles is a conundrum that is definitely held by the wisdom of God. Why some get healed and some do not (or not yet) is a mystery. What each healing does do, though, is provide a unique glance into a God who never stops working on our behalf. Whether it be super-miracles or non-creative miracles, God's hand is at work, constantly exercising his faithfulness and power towards our lives. More power to those who believe it!

The Myth of More Faith

5

The Failure of Faith

Not everything we're actually 'believing God for' eventuates. People say that God is an eleventh-hour God, in that he comes through just in the nick of time. That's often true, but at times he comes through at 2:45 p.m. the next day (too late for the success of *our* plan A, but obviously committed to the success of *his* plan A). Sometimes, however, it's too late in every respect for God to seemingly come through . . . either the person's died, or irreversible decisions had to be made in the absence of the obvious intervention of God.

The usual answer given to this is the person mustn't have had enough faith. This may be the case for some, but making such blanket statements, is on a par with CSI New York claiming death by arsenic every time there's a murder. It's worth considering the following other reasons why prayers at times were not answered, such as:

1. God never gave a specific word of faith

Our faith is generally obtained by a revelation of God's nature, not his plans. We believe that God is a provider but we usually don't get a specific word about his particular way of providing. Because faith comes by hearing (Rom. 10:17) and God never tricks us, it would seem that we frequently attach our faith to something God never said. To put God in a half nelson and demand that he should provide something specific that he never particularly promised is a recipe for a mini breakdown! When it fails to come to pass, neither God nor our faith has failed us. It is impossible for either to ever happen. What actually happened was that what we hoped for failed, not what we 'believed' for. We still believe he is our provider.

Our church's commitment to church planting is driven by a word about church planting, yet, whilst our second church plant in East Yorkshire failed, the 'word' we'd got had not. The Spirit of the Word led us to go on to plant in Manchester, Leeds, Liverpool, Newcastle and Birmingham. His word has never failed, even though we have had a good number of failures; our failures were on the way to seeing God's word eventually come to pass!

2. It hasn't failed – its time just has not come

Faith is usually tested. For Abraham, the tests were carried out over twenty-five years! For Job, some say less than a year. Abraham's tests included:

* The familiarity test – leaving all that was familiar
* The famine test – things got worse before they got better
* The first shall be last test – Lot got the best of the land
* The first fruit test – what you do when you first succeed (the meeting with Melchizedek)
* The fruition test – how long do we have to wait?
* The funeral test – when the dream must die and faith becomes trust

Generally, when God speaks to us and faith is released, it is still accompanied by much enthusiasm and earthly support. Faith is then stripped back until it is the only thing left standing. It is there that faith, the size of a mustard seed, obtains its promise.

3. We give up five minutes before the miracle

Faith didn't fail us, we failed it. Because faith requires obedience in order to verify its credentials, and in order to reposition us in the place where miracles happen, our disobedience can be a major contributing factor to its seeming lack of results. Most words of faith come without a time schedule attached, but we often add a sell-by date to the promise that is before God's appointed time. Discouragement, despondency and doubt can all be contributing factors.

4. Other people are to blame!

Because we've made faith individualistic – it's all about my believing – all of the blame is placed on me when my plans fail. The story of the four men who helped the paraplegic through the roof above where Jesus was teaching sheds a different light on things. It says 'When Jesus saw their faith, he said, "Friend, your sins are forgiven"' (Luke 5:20). It was the corporate faith of the team which healed their crippled friend. If that's the case, our neglect of other people's issues could be to blame for their lack of power and breakthrough. It pays to walk a little humbly.

5. God withheld the miracle

Our 'faith' went outside of the bounds of faith when we believed for stuff that was beyond our maturity level. If we have only dealt in hundreds of pounds, the obvious next step is to believe for thousands of pounds, not millions. It is rare that God ever takes people from nothing to everything in one huge leap. Usually it's the 'steps of a good man' (Ps. 37: 23, KJV) that prevail. Steps take into account our increasing maturity levels and our ability to handle responsibilities. God is Father, not just a miracle assistant.

6. God has a higher plan

Sometimes faith fails because of what I have termed 'the default button' of God. His ways remain higher than our ways and his dreams, ambitions and direction for our lives are always deeper, wider and higher than we could ever imagine. Often God takes the failure of our faith and turns it into a divine success. When Jim

Elliot was slaughtered through his attempts to save the Auca Indians of South America, his death led to the rise of hundreds of missionaries looking to take his place. This led to the eventual breakthrough of the gospel into the South American dark interior.

Out of the persecution, death and confiscation of property by Mao Tse-tung in the mid-twentieth century, China has seen an unprecedented uprising of Christians even in the midst of continued suppression. The saying remains true that 'the blood of the martyrs is the seed of the church' (Tertullian).

Because you can't make faith up, it's simplistic and primitive to say that things failed purely for lack of it. A lack of results, as we have seen, may not be our fault. People continue to say, 'If you only believed more.' It's OK to say, 'If only we doubted less', but it's not OK to say, 'If only we believed more.' You cannot regulate belief. You can't psych yourself into believing any more than you can psych yourself a miracle. Often it's not through a lack of faith that plans fail, it's through an *absence* of faith, and it must therefore be said that those plans may never have actually been the plans of destiny. It's important to add that my musings refer to people who have really opened their heart and mind to God and really desire his very best in their lives. In that way, the faith God wants to be deposited in their hearts is deposited, the absence of faith being a 'God thing' and not a 'sin thing'.

The Myth of Sincerity

How Being Two-Faced Can Really Work For You

The two faces that people often put on are a 'long face' and a 'face like thunder'. And it's all in the name of honesty and sincerity! People often think that in being real and authentic they have permission to be super-grumpy, super-irritable, and generally very unattractive.

I'm definitely not one for 'Plastic Fantastics' where everyone flashes their permanent smiles and hides the 'real them', but I'm also worried about what we allow ourselves to be in the name of sincerity. People are starting to give sincerity a bad name! In the words of Simon McIntyre from C3 Church in Sydney, 'Sincerity has become an overrated sentiment'.[7] He's not challenging the tenures of honesty and openness, but challenging the liberty we give ourselves to be horrible by claiming that we're just 'being ourselves'! If that's the case, there's a strong case, both socially and spiritually, for being 'two-faced'.

The real truth is that if you've had the privilege and honour of becoming a Christian through putting Jesus on the centre stage of your life and loving him with all your heart, a very real thing happens – you get 'born again'. Your heart becomes new and the Holy Spirit makes his home within you. In 2 Corinthians 5:17 it says: 'Therefore, if anyone is in Christ, he is a new creation; the old has gone, the new has come!' Our old self or heart has been crucified with Christ and our new self has been raised with Christ (see Rom. 6).

OK – that's the technical bit over! Here's the practical bit. When someone comes to me and says, 'Can I be honest with you?' I fear the worst. I figure that I'm about to have a truckload of disappointment, discontentment and general disarray tipped all over my lap. It may be honest with how the person feels, yet it's often not honest with the real state of their new hearts, and the transforming and active work of the Holy Spirit. To be really, *really* honest, they would have to start with 'Jesus reigns and all things are working for our good' (see Rom. 8:28) and they'd at least have to conclude with 'We're going to make it and I think God's brilliant'. A big YES for real sincerity!

Being sincere to emotion is OK; being sincere to circumstances is OK – yet it is not the basis of a powerful life of an overcomer who draws strength down from heaven and breaks through to new levels of success and victory. That comes from sincerity to faith and the Word of God. Emotional sincerity must be tempered by real truth.

There is a time for a healthy disclosure of pent-up emotion, but it should be kept in the private place of either your personal devotion or, on rare occasions, your inner circle of loved ones who aren't offended by your rattiness. Usually your emotions never carry with them the whole truth or the right truth and that's why, when flaunted under the guise of sincerity, they become detrimental and often destructive. It only takes a few seconds of vindictive honesty to cut someone's head off. It takes a lot longer, however, to sew it back on and even then, it doesn't quite swivel the way it used to.

Put It On

Colossians 3:12 says, 'Therefore, as God's chosen people, holy and dearly loved, clothe yourselves with compassion, kindness, humility, gentleness and patience.'

It encourages us to *put it on*. Putting it on is often not seen as an attribute, yet it's encouraged by the Word of God. Taking off the spirit of heaviness and putting on the garments of praise is a pretty biblical thing to do. Taking off the old self and putting on the new is also quite biblical.

It's true that more often than not, I'm actually putting it on. People often say about themselves, 'I'm a shy person.' Well, why not become a people person by 'putting on' courage and an over-whelming interest in other people? That's what I attempt to do, especially on Sundays! People say that they don't feel that they're an 'up' kind of person. Well, be 'up' by putting on joy and peace in the Holy Spirit. You can do it with Christ's strength.

The Bible never encourages us to put on misery, grumpiness, faithlessness, cruelty, unkindness, sulkiness or bitterness. It does tell us to be true to who we are. If you've been set free in your heart from the pain and guilt of sin, it's time to be true to who you really are! You may feel down in the dumps, yet your real state of play is 'blessed . . . with every spiritual blessing' (Eph. 1:3). I don't want to sound triumphalistic, but I do feel as if we have slightly misinter-preted the mantra of today – 'I just want to be myself.'

Stick a BUT in It

The greatest word I've found in my Bible that actually unites feel-ings with faith and helps us to be genuinely two-faced – the face of our soul (our mind, emotions and humanity) united with the face of our spirit (the place of victory in Christ) – is the word 'BUT'. There is no sharper use of the word than in Psalm 31. The psalmist David writes:

> I am forgotten by them as though I were dead;
> I have become like broken pottery.
> For I hear the slander of many;

there is terror on every side;
they conspire against me
and plot to take my life.
BUT I trust in you, O LORD;
I say, 'You are my God.'
My times are in your hands.
(vv. 12–15a, my emphasis)

His emotions are real and yet they are superseded by a higher reality – God is his refuge, strength and support. 'BUT' is a word that has been invented to usher in information that had previously been blocked out. It puts sincerity with emotions in perspective by placing it alongside the deeper truth of the Word of God.

Try it today! After putting your feelings through the filter of 'Is it really helpful for those around me to know this?' and 'Is airing my feelings just an excuse to be self-centred and self-pitying?' you can positively attach them to the powerful word of truth that promises never to return empty but to accomplish all it was sent and purposed to achieve (Isa. 55:11).

Can you 'just be yourself' and 'be true to who you are'? Sure you can, but get used to being better, speaking better and looking better than how you feel. It's time to grab your 'BUT' and get moving!

PART 2:

SACRED COWS IN THE CHURCH WORLD

The years have been kind to you.
It's the weekends that have done the damage.

Anon

Introduction

One of the things that bug me about church life is that a lot of the work is done by only a small percentage of the people. Many times people have come up to me and told me that we should pray more. However, when I put on that special prayer meeting – they're nowhere to be seen! In this section, I look at this inequality as well as how the divisions within the English football league reflect the different levels of commitment and motivations within the church you're a part of right now.

If someone asks me to pass the baton again, I'm just going to shout 'no'! There's pressure on every side to raise up successors, pressure to see growth in season and out, pressure to keep up with the latest manifestations, as well as pressure to close the back door of the church through unreal pastoral care. I've been wondering if it's the pressure of the Holy Spirit or if it's possibly the pressure leaders put on themselves to keep up with the expectations of some very naughty sacred cows!

In Part 2, we look at:

The Myth of Equal Sacrifice
The Myth of Belong, Believe, Dream and Achieve
The Myth of the Next Generation
The Myth of Destiny

It's time for the church to find a new confidence in who it is and to ward off the holy cows that want to trample their dangerous hooves all over the real truths about church life and growth. It's time to put another cow on the barbie!

The Myth of Equal Sacrifice

The 80/20 Rule – Break It at Your Peril!

There is a rule that churches and their leaders are constantly trying to break – it's the 80/20 rule. Good luck! I believe that it's a universal rule and has never been broken in business, colleges or voluntary organizations anywhere in the world – ever. And it's not about to be broken now by you!

Right now, the church I pastor is in the middle of a vision to raise £1 million for the future 'Megaplex' facility, by creating wealth through investments, creativity and sacrifice. So far, though, my wife Jenny and my personal pledge amounts to around one twentieth of the total. With far more than twenty couples in our church, and some much wealthier people than us, our pledge seems way out of perspective. It's not fair, but it is right in that God isn't looking for equal giving or equal sacrifice. To those who have received more revelation – more sacrifice is expected. It's the unbreakable rule that lies under every facet of church, business and social life – the 80/20 rule. It says that 80 per cent of all the work done comes from 20 per cent of the people; 80 per cent of all gifts, talents, passion, enthusiasm and energy comes from just 20 per cent of the people, and it's not necessarily the richest 20 per cent. It's leaders – not in function but in heart – that cause it all to be so disproportionate. If the bulk of the people rise up more, 'leadership' rises even more. If the masses catch up with the leaders at any time, the leaders speed off even deeper into the territory of not just unequal giving, but unequal sacrifice. That's what sets them apart. If it doesn't, the rule takes over – someone else will overtake them and they'll no longer be the leaders.

Jesus, unlike overly desperate leaders such as me at times, never attempted to break the rule. He never begged anyone to rise out of mediocrity. In fact, one startling moment of transparency can be found in Mark 4:11,12:

> He told them, 'The secret of the kingdom of God has been given to you. But to those on the outside everything is said in parables so that, 'they may be ever seeing but never perceiving, and ever hearing but never understanding; otherwise they might turn and be forgiven!'

Parables were not only meant to reveal truth – they were meant to disguise and hide the truth. Jesus gave this revelation in the midst of a kingdom revelation about the parable of the sower. Even though some seed fell on hard, shallow and overcrowded soil, it wasn't the principal intent of the farmer. It was good seed for good soil. All else was wasted. The ministry of Jesus was to open hearts – not close them. The difference doesn't lie in outer goodness or inner goodness, but in simple faith and honest humility. Jesus was not a beggar. The antidote of salvation cost him his blood. The pearl of great price is only for people who value it. It is the sole property of the sincere and the hungry. Sure, he died for all, but it is only accessible to some.

As a leader of a church, I have spent years begging the hard-hearted to attend conferences, prayer meetings, Wednesday night cell groups, men's nights, women's nights, youth nights and Sunday nights. All of that has ceased – well, all except for the occasional panic attack originating from vivid dreams of not one single person turning up to the forthcoming event!

How many leaders have taken themselves to the point of exhaustion and stress trying to break the 80/20 rule? When trying to undo the law of gravity, you do it at your own peril. Here are five reasons why begging (or even whipping) never works, and why you need to once again give respect to the mighty 80/20.

1. Begging replaces vision

No one is inspired by a beggar. When I did my 'Great British Generosity Experiment' on the streets of London a number of years ago, I dressed up as a beggar to find out how much money beggars actually make on the streets of London. Soon after sitting down with my cap in hand I got arrested and charged for the illegal act of begging. (So I won't be doing it again any time soon.) After being released from a police cell, I put on some Hawaiian clothes and went out to raise money for a charity in Devon. Later, I borrowed a suit from Savoy Tailoring and did the same thing, only this time I was looking like a million dollars. The difference in response was as night and day. As a super-cheeky charity worker I made four times more than as a cheeky charity worker, and forty times more than as a low-key, depressed charity worker!

Stay away from 'if everyone could give £10' or 'if everyone could give an hour a month' . . . it never works and never will. To raise an army, you've got to raise the stakes. Envision. Call to the cause. Inspire. Just don't take the designer label off the greatest cause in the world and sell it at Matalan or Primark prices. Begging, calling people to a sense of duty, selling it cheap, can't break the 80/20 rule, but certainly causes it to be an anaemic reflection of those who play to the strength of the role – those who lead by vision, inspiration and opportunity. A visionary leader still has 20 per cent of the people doing 80 per cent of the work but, like a balloon that's being blown up, both the 20 per cent and 80 per cent represent far more people than those following the uninspiring leader. The 20 per cent may give 80 per cent of the offerings, yet under the visionary leader the overall offerings are drastically higher than that of the non-visionary leader.

2. Begging replaces faith

To beg Jesus is right. To beg people is wrong. If you want a husband to remain an unbeliever, keep leaving those tracts in the bedroom. If you want your 19-year-olds to stay in the shadows, keep harassing them with church flyers and open Bibles. If you want your church to be earth-bound, carnal, emotive and spoilt – keep begging. The only ingredient for breakthrough is faith. Faith refuses to beg; it's persistent at heaven's gates, it fails to give up, it knows what it wants; it asks, seeks and knocks . . . but never begs. Faith is often initially accompanied by a loss of people and a loss of support – ask Gideon, David, Moses and even Jesus when you're next in heaven!

3. Begging loses dignity

You can't keep your dignity and lie down on street corners, yet so many believers are found pleading with people to go to church, join a team, be at the prayer meeting or even come to the social. If they simply don't want to, your pleading will make them 'want to' even less.

For years after their separation, I watched my mother become subservient to my father in order to win back his heart and regain his hand in marriage. In doing so, she lost not only valuable time that she could have spent building a stronger personal life, but also a degree of respect. She lost her appeal. Relationally, playing hard to get actually increases appeal. It regains the mystique that's missing in a lot of relationships. Every time Jesus becomes really familiar to us, he surprises us by doing something unexpected, or by simply being a little mysterious . . . like when he was transfigured in a private showing to some of his disciples on a mountainside. Great leaders are not completely accessible. They say 'follow me' and leave it up to the desire of the listener whether they do or don't. They don't stay around for long before they move to the next thing. They don't kowtow to the late adaptors. They persevere and create dignity – they add value to themselves by adding value to their call and cause, and so attract the visionaries who love the challenge of a new experience.

4. Begging reverses leadership

Church life is all about raising Sons of the House. Unless there are some hurdles to jump, money to pay and prayers to pray, how can a leader really tell the difference between sons and servants? Isn't that what midweek meetings do? They sort out the sons from the servants. Begging people to do things confuses the picture. To ask people twice to be a part of your brilliant steward's team (and to be refused twice) is permissible, but to ask three times is begging. You may get the people, but they become your leader, you become their servant. Better a small team of great people than a larger team of people who wouldn't be there if it had not been for the visit, the email, the text . . . and the congratulations even after a poor, dismal display of effortless assistance.

In the parable of the wedding banquet (Matt. 22:1–14), the king only ever sent his servants out twice to tell them who had been invited to his son's wedding which was about to begin. There was no third invitation. The invitation was then cast out to the highways and byways.

5. Begging doesn't change hearts

No matter how much you plead, bleed, beg or push, you cannot change a human heart. And without heart change, even if you do get them to church or to the prayer meeting, they'll only come once and never again.

The only one that can open the door to a change of heart is them. Honesty is a decision. Humility is a decision. Belief is a decision. Without those decisions to offload lies, pride and sarcasm, there is nothing that can change people.

After running a one-year training school for over a decade, I can't recall one person who was changed by it who didn't firstly change themselves from secretive to open and from cynical to simple. Faith and humility are the two front doors that God enters through in order to exercise his life-changing power. He surely can change a heart of stone to a heart of flesh, but only when there's a double door into that heart. Otherwise he will not – and, according to the life of Jesus, won't spend time trying to. A man convinced to do something against his will is still of the same mind. A woman pushed to buy a dress never wears it.

Those who respect the 80/20 rule know where to put most of their time and effort – into the 20 per cent. They know where most of the fruit will come from – the faith-filled and the 'early adaptors'. They sniff out Gideon's 300 in the midst of Gideon's 30,000. They look for the seventy out of the crowd, the twelve out of the seventy, and the three out of the twelve. They're smart. They know that 80/20 is here to stay. Oh, and by the way, great leaders don't try to make it 90/10! To get 10 per cent of the people to do 90 per cent of the work is to (again) try to bend the rule. The outcome is a blip of extra activity for the 10 per cent . . . then burnout! Stick with the 80/20, add vision, add some enthusiasm and watch the results!

The Myth of Belong, Believe, Dream and Achieve

The Premier League – Not Everyone's in It

Just like the English football scene, churches are filled with people who play in the Premier League, the Championship League, League One, League Two, and a large number that only play in the Pub League on Sundays. The Premier League comprises the 20 per cent of Christians that both create and sustain the indomitable 80/20 rule of church life.

Most Christians think that they're Premier League players when actually they're not. They express their love for God in the language of the Premier League, but their lives speak of a league that requires a little or a lot less than this league does.

The Premier League is exclusive. Jesus described this league many times in Luke 9:57–62. Three men told him that they'd follow him wherever he went. Jesus set a high benchmark. To one he said, 'Foxes have holes, birds have nests, but I don't have a home (on earth that is).' To another he said, 'Let the dead bury their own dead', and to another, 'Whoever puts his hand to the plough and looks back isn't fit for the kingdom of God.' Jesus was relentless and inflexible in his requirements for discipleship. It had to be pretty immediate; it was to be absolutely continuous and needed to be the number one priority. Even the rich young ruler had to sell everything, not just most things. Now, that's harsh! It is, however, the high standard of the Premiership.

Again, the Law of Hard

Jesus was, of course, not dealing with external issues. He was dealing with heart dispositions – he was challenging the willingness of the heart. The Premier League is characterized not by degrees of holiness or knowledge, but by openness to change. It's for people 'on the curve' – the learning curve, that is. It's for people who are being transformed from glory to glory. People who put life through the filter of 'Endure hardship as discipline' (Heb. 12:7), rather than 'encountering hardship is of the devil.'

'Hard' becomes the opportunity for growth, and growth means change. Opposition is the sand that creates the pearls for Premier League Christians. Instead of reacting to circumstances, they use circumstances for their own development. Why? Because they're people 'on the curve'.

Not everyone in your church is 'on the curve'. Many are not changing. Many are content with either surviving or simply enjoying the dividends of Christianity. Many are not 'early adaptors'. They follow only when a majority of people start following the new direction of the Spirit. They often say that things are 'too hard' and therefore fail to become overcomers. They want the mountains beyond to move and are oblivious to the inner mountains of the heart that need to be moved first. They often say that they've been hurt and state that as their reason for not vigorously pursuing vision.

Let's Get Motivated

Jesus told his enquirers that in order to follow him fully, they needed to love God with all their 'heart . . . soul . . . mind and . . . strength' (Mark 12:30). This defines the four motivational areas of life. With the heart, one believes. With the soul, one belongs. With the mind, one thinks and dreams. And with strength, one achieves.

Jesus declared that they had to love God with all they believed, with all their sense of belonging, with all their dreaming and all their achieving. Jesus wasn't just giving four areas of surrender – he was giving a priority package of surrender: *believe, belong, dream and achieve.*

The Premier League

The Premier League begins with believing and surrenders all other issues to their faith in God. They're led by being called by God and not by feelings of acceptance or rejection, hurt or relief. For those in the Premiership, faith is 360 degrees. It not only has faith for the future but also faith for the past. It sees that even the injustices of the past as launch sites for fresh revelations from God and clings on to Romans 8:28: 'And we know that in all things God works for the good of those who love him, who have been called according to his purpose.'

These Premier players have the freedom to pass the ball, the skill to curve the ball and the undivided attention to shoot the ball accurately to see God's kingdom advance.

The Championship League

Some say that people need to belong, believe, dream and achieve, in that order. They say that to build a great church, a sense of belonging needs to be the top priority. That's true for the Championship League, but not for the Premier League. The Premier League is to do with believing first, not belonging. If believing comes first, it's the calling of God that drives the ship, not the fellowship and friendship with all the other travellers. You can build a great church in the Championship but it cannot be sustained. Belonging without full believing works when people feel wanted and needed. Most people leave churches because 'no one loves them'. That's the weakness of the Championship League. Just go to America and see the inhaling and exhaling of people simply because they lose a sense of belonging and a new church down the road now offers a truckload of the stuff. The new church soon becomes the old church and the cycle moves on.

League One

If the Championship League is driven by a need to belong, with a need to believe coming a good yet poor second, League One is driven by a need to think the same and dream the same as the church they attend. It's a cognitive understanding that leads the League One players. They want to be able to visualize the future of the church, and they want to put their stamp of agreement on all that's about to take place.

So many churches now put on DNA classes in order to outline the vision and values of their particular fellowship. Sincere in motive and helpful in measure, these classes do little to enthuse the Premier League players who recognize that 99 per cent of the DNA of their church is Jesus and not its five-year goal, new building project, new missions venture or unique blend of coffee! League One players are very interested in all of this because they lack the inner dynamic of change and knowledge that characterizes the Premier League. They're looking to agree and then submit. They're looking to have their dream life stimulated by the unfolding of large plans.

Most vision courses have been put on to appease the League One players. They make very little long-term difference to the success of the vision. The real vision is Jesus, and that firstly takes revelation, not a mental ascent. League One players will run with a vision that ignites their mental and imaginary juices but, when the vision loses the pizzazz of big building projects and large projected growth, they soon lose interest.

When someone wants me to explain our vision and there's a pressure to have to give them some kind of one-year, two-year and five-year goal, I resist by saying, 'I don't know.' It's not that I don't know anything, but it's a resistance to build the church on mental ascent rather than a belief in God's sovereignty, calling and covenant. If I know that it's a Premier League player doing the asking it's quite a different matter. For them it's belief first, but they also have to have their imagination ignited by the faith they possess. I'm not eradicating vision, just trying to sanctify it by submitting it to the power of revelation. In the past, when I've fallen under the pressure from 'dream chasers', I tended to make up our vision and goals. None of them ever came to pass, but nobody noticed because no one who heard them ever stuck around long enough to know either way! (Goals are like the dental floss of church life. They help keep the cutting edge intact, but are not absolutely necessary. It's our role to plant diligently, expect greatly and believe unswervingly. Goals can help the process, but one thing we can't do is control outcomes. Growth still belongs to God.)

League Two

If the Premier League is driven by believing, the Championship by belonging, League One by dreaming and agreeing, then League Two is driven by achievement.

As long as they are involved in something that is being rewarded by either results or praise, this league remains satisfied. I see myself as an achiever. I'm performance driven. It becomes an asset to the church only when submitted to the spirit of faith and trust. Without yielding, the spirit of achievement leads easily to the spirit of striving. It creates a 'self-made' church with all of the right programmes and activities but without the stamp of the Holy Spirit's authorization on it. It becomes like a house built of wood, hay and stubble. It can look amazing, but it cannot withstand the fires that rage from time to time.

Many people who are driven by huge gusts of energy and enthusiasm tend to eventually die in despondency and despair unless quickly redirected back to faith and trust. A lot of churches burn out through pandering to the spirit of high achievement. The wolf comes and blows the house down.

Loving God with all of your 'strength' is to submit this need to achieve to the need to believe. There are many times in church life where things take a turn for the worse when the attendance drops, the leadership team is reduced in size and plans are put on hold. It's at these times where 'strength' is urged to come under 'belief' and is therefore sanctified and made holy. Afterwards, its relentless energy becomes a huge asset to the church.

If you build a League Two church, it will be brilliant when the going is good, but when the going gets tough, hold on – you're in for an even tougher ride than expected.

The Pub League

The lowest of all the leagues is the Pub League that just meets on a Sunday. Its driving force is attendance. It has no real interest in faith, belonging, dreaming or achievement. It simply wants to relieve a little bit of guilt either put there by religion or by the Holy Spirit. The 'players' still lift their hands from time to time, and sometimes pluck up the courage to say 'amen'. They are the periphery of church life. It is everyone's hope that they will eventually add faith to their outings and become a part of the brilliant Premier League. In the meantime, they should be cared for but not discipled. Many pastors and church leaders run themselves ragged trying to disciple people who have no intention of submitting their lives under the mighty hand of God.

In Acts 20:28, Paul urges the Ephesians elders to 'Keep watch over yourselves and all the flock of which the Holy Spirit has made you overseers.' The problems come when we keep watch over all those who are grazing with the flock, who look like the flock, but exhibit distinctly 'un-flock-like' behaviour the more you get to know them. With all respect to the animal kingdom, you can't build a church on goats!

Payment by Instalments

All five leagues are in operation in every church. They're more defined today than in the Early Church because our society's way of paying for stuff is by instalments, rather than by full payment. Our churches today are designed with ramps from community to core, rather than steep ledges, because the payment requirements are gradual. People can, however, go straight from League Two to Premier League, simply by paying the full cost of allowing their heart to become a heart of faith and a heart after change. They don't necessarily have to stop smoking straight away or immediately get married to their long-term partner. That will all happen through inner change and outer obedience. They just have to really *want* to change. 'Changing' or 'being transformed' leads people on a journey of discovery – discovering more about God and his ways. Revelation almost always comes after obedience. Obedience is our response to what God has already said. Premier League Christianity is simply about doing the last thing he said to do; not just our favourite thing to do. It's costly but it creates powerful churches.

In accepting the five leagues of church life, and in not watering down the Premier League, it is possible to create an awesome church that's powerful in all four of its motivational areas – heart, soul, mind and strength.

Firstly, after focusing on the foundation of faith, it spends time on a sense of belonging (through small groups and welcome teams), a sense of going somewhere (through goals and vision statements) and a sense of achievement (through roles and functions). Believing and conviction is what God builds his church on, and in realizing this, leaders can create empowered people who stand on the foundation of surrender. Only then will the church remain continuously strong.

Secondly, it allows people to drop out of the Premier League without being thrown into the 'sin bin'. Jesus had high standards for the Premier League, but also respected people's right to choose. He didn't berate them, argue with them or seduce them. He spoke simply and sparingly. To accept various leagues outside of the Premier League is to accept people's right to choose. When they choose to do so, they can return to or go straight to the Premier League without passing through all the other leagues. It says that fellowship, vision and achievement are good things, but leaves space for what is the greatest thing – faith in God's sovereignty, God's lordship and God's callings.

No Pressure

It's imperative that a church nurtures Premier League players, but never pressures people to become one. When people are pushed into Premier League Christianity without the necessary pliable heart, they are pressured into faking it and spend their time 'keeping up appearances'. This always leads to friction and eventual separation. All of our leadership should come from the Premier League, but not all of the Premier League are official leaders. It provides a pool for both current and emerging leaders. If you're reading this book, you're most probably in the Premier League – not because of the excellence of my book but because you are displaying the signs of wanting to learn more about the real workings and wisdom of God. Teachability, along with a willingness to start afresh, is all a part of what makes the Premier League what it is.

Churches that experience a steroidal form of church growth through the enticement of a great vision, great teen programme, great music or even a great leader, often find that a season of church in-fighting and splitting follows. Because all key leaders of a church ought to be selected from the Premier League, these churches split because many leaders were selected directly from the other leagues. Church splits often result because of the variation of the purity of the heart motivation across the leadership team.

Pastoral Pursuits

Discernment is important, especially when creating a team that leads a church or a ministry into its future. 'Out of . . . [the heart flows] the issues of life' (Prov. 4:23, KJV) is as pertinent for the heart of the church as for the heart of an individual. Out of the leadership team will come a church or ministry that reflects it.

In many cases, it's important for team leaders to be pre-emptive in their repositioning of some team members who have cooled down and are now failing to be 'on the curve'. To allow these to remain is to eventually create friction and fall out. To seek another role for them that removes them from the 'heart' is to respect their inner decision to stop growing with the pace of the church or ministry, as well as to love them into a 'lesser' – but still 'important' – role. It places them in a less demanding yet respected division from which they can leap-frog back into the Premier League if they so choose.

The apostle Paul once made an outlandish comment that shows his understanding of the church league divisions. He claimed that even if people preached the gospel out of 'envy . . . [or] rivalry', they should be allowed to do so for the sake of the gospel being preached (Phil. 1:15–18). Here he describes the Pub League – people whose hearts are cold, but they still have an affiliation with the message of Christ. They may be overweight with sin but at least they come on Sunday. Grace needs to be bountifully applied to church life without a watering down of what creates the power and dynamics of the life of every church – the Premier League.

The Myth of the Next Generation

Whatever You Do – Don't Pass the Baton

I don't like it when people start talking about 'passing the baton' to the next generation. I'm not doing it. It's not that I'm insecure and it's not that I don't respect those who herald it, but I'm simply not going there. The only place I can see that happening in Scripture is when someone's about to die! I'm not planning on it, so I'm not creating the ultimate plan for it.

If you want to devalue and demobilize a band of believers, then go ahead. Get them to pass their one solitary baton to some young gun and be left standing on the sidelines simply and dutifully cheering on the next generation. 'Cheering on' may be lacking in many quarters of church life, but the last thing I want to create with the over-40s is just a cheer squad. You can still cheer while you're running.

The truth of the matter is this – there is no such thing as 'the baton'. There is a baton that's to be held by everyone in their various stages of life development but there isn't one *solitary* baton. It's absolutely true that as we move from, say, living in our twenties to living in our thirties, we pass on a certain baton which includes lifestyle, mindset and anointing – but we then take a new baton which includes a new lifestyle, mindset and anointing. Everyone has a race to run and everyone has a baton to hold. The 4 x 4 baton (relay race) analogy of church life falls flat on its face the moment the one baton is handed on. In real church living, another one instantly appears.

It all comes out of our desperation to get younger people into church life. What we really want, however, is everyone to play their part. I can recall one day seeing my dad dancing to Abba by himself when he was in his fifties. (It was at the time when Abba was the hippest thing around.) Now, that was odd. And it is odd in church life to have people in their different life stages exhibiting behaviour that is not becoming to that particular stage of life. 'Dad-dancing' every night should not be encouraged if the dad is serious about the new season of life he's now in.

For people in their twenties, going to bed at 10 p.m. should also be not encouraged! 'Being sensible' and 'balance' are not terms that the iPod generation should understand. 'Excess' is their real middle name, with that excess being channelled into excessive passion for the house of God and the message of Christ. Outside of being a newish Christian, people in their forties who play guitar in the church band and who aren't training anyone else up to play along with them (or instead of them) should also have a good talking to! If you're in your forties, a big part of your role is to impart your skill and wisdom to the emerging generation.

The reason why church life is so mixed up is because worldly value systems have infiltrated the hearts of many. If your church publicly promotes people in their twenties, you'll usually find a dip in the number of people in their forties, and an accompanying rise of people in their fifties. Without re-education and the introduction of a new value system and a new baton, those in their forties are often jealous of those in their twenties. They used to lead worship – now some good-looking 20-year-old has got the job. They used to be in the Leadership Academy under the optimistic gaze of the senior pastor – now a whole new class attends and, guess what, they're all 20-something. Without a change of mandate, the 40-somethings either:

1. Leave the church and join a much smaller breakaway where they're needed on the drums
2. Develop a sneering attitude and work against the progress of the new hotshots or
3. Have a midlife crisis and look for excitement that is outside of the boundaries of righteousness

Many of those in their fifties, however, have children now in their twenties, and so become fans of those in their twenties – that's if the 50-somethings make it through their forties, and that's a big 'if'. Baton dropping is easy to do. If you add to the dilemma that Mr 40-something knows that his 50-something boss or 50-something spiritual leader is looking to 'pass the baton' to someone in their thirties, then no wonder that, without proper values and vision, the forties have become notorious for midlife crises.

The real challenge of church is to guard and promote the transitions between the different stages of life that everyone is destined to pass through. It requires each of us to reinvent ourselves for the new stage of life. Just as a tree loses its autumn leaves in order to gain a new set, everyone who wants long-term success must pass on the mandate of their previous life stage, and pick up the mandate and identity of their new stage of life.

In the following, I identify six stages of life as well as the lifestyles, mindsets and vision that accompany each of those stages. I also identify the vulnerabilities of each stage and the baton that each receives and gives as they pass through each life stage. It must be said that these life stages I have outlined follow tracks of life experienced by many, but not by everyone. They take the journey of someone who has been brought up in the faith or come into the faith at an early age. I plot the natural progression of teen, young adult, young married, married with kids and empty nesters, and mirror this progression with a spiritual progression throughout the church. (Because many people get saved beyond the teen years, these life stages can almost step on each other from time to time – for example, someone saved in their forties could exhibit both some of the characteristics of 20-somethings as well as those of the 40-somethings.) Here are the six stages I've identified.

Stage One: Teen Years

I would say that the baton of the teen years is 'Discovery Time'. The call is for teenagers to move from parental belief or preconceived beliefs to original belief, and the process is that of discovering God for themselves. Discovering who they really are is fought on a mine-field of sexual consciousness, image consciousness and peer pressure. We need more teens in church. We need to give them room to fail, room to mess up and room to rediscover the true essence of Jesus without the trimmings and trappings of our religion.

Stage Two: The Twenties

The baton of the twenties generation is 'Born to Run'. The twenties is the decade of passion. For those who were saved from the teen years or earlier, it's where the belief of the earlier years becomes hard-nosed conviction. To successfully navigate this ten-year span, there must be a commitment to excess and we must provide a church environment where the 20-somethings can be excessive. There used to be a name for those who worked for our church at our building called The Megacentre – they were called 'Megaholics'. It was a term that light-heartedly described the attitude of most of the young adults that worked there – full on and addicted! That's the birthright for anyone in their twenties. The flip side is the world's binge culture of excess. Being a sexually charged generation, it's important that the 20-somethings find themselves in the right place at the right time, absorbed with destiny and purpose. Without it there's often a whole lot of relational trouble as they invest their energies more into natural desires rather than spiritual quests. The cutting edge is the only place to be in the twenties.

Stage Three: The Thirties

The baton of the thirties generation could well be 'We are the Champions'. These years are potentially strong years to champion and lead the cause of Christ. The thirties represent the championing of a new age of religion-free Christianity – utterly opposed to past regimes and dogmas. It also represents the time of intensely raising a family that becomes the heir of the culture and convictions ushered in by the thirties generation.

The transition into the thirties is met hard with the devil's aim to distract the main breadwinner with an obsession with ladder-climbing, and discourage the main child-carer with feelings of uselessness and abandonment. The new age needs champions – and this decade of believer is to be just that.

Stage Four: The Forties

The baton of the forties generation is 'Pillars of Strength'. There's a general but by no means universal transition here from front of house to behind the scenes – just as an actor of the main stage can become a producer of the stage show. Behind every performer is a room of directors, producers and leaders – and that's the same with the workings of God's church. For those who have been a part of church life for a significant length of time, the transition from limelight to lowlight can be the hardest to make for some – but it is the most important. Envy of those in their twenties can thwart the process. Insecurity can abound. Yet, if the twenties represent passion and energy, the thirties represent championing of new ideas and programmes, then the forties are there to give strength – pillars of it.

With usually less time available than those in their twenties, but more than those in their thirties, it's important to act strategically, entrusting their wisdom to reliable people who will in turn do the same. Pillars don't win awards, yet without them the roof would collapse. Let everyone in their forties rise up and start to carry the weight of the church financially, emotionally, strategically and prayerfully. If we are in our forties, we should quit feeling rejected, quit cynicism, quit quitting. It's time for pillars of strength to rise!

Stage Five: The Fifties

The principal baton of the fifties generation is 'Carers of People'. So often in charismatic churches, the badge of leadership is taken off someone in their fifties and placed on someone in their thirties. The main temptation for those in their fifties is to invent ways of being significant once again instead of holding on to their incredible value to the Body of Christ. Maturity should bring about a completeness of identity in Christ, rather than a loss of identity. The fifties is about spiritual parenting, not spiritual consumerism.

The fifties can also be a huge reinvention time that includes some kind of re-education, getting stuff out that was packed away during the 'young family' years, as well as making brand-new friendships and acquaintances.

Stage Six: The Sixties (and beyond!)

The baton of the sixties generation is 'Guardians of the Vision'. For those who have been saved for quite some time and with years of wisdom and love, it's essential that those in this generation never neglect the power of oversight, and see it as their role to not just care for the flock, but to see the next stage of life for everyone successfully transitioned into and every part of church life thrive.

Without the dogma of those in their thirties, without some of the workload of those in their forties and without the particular concerns of those in their fifties, the sixties can provide the wisdom and power to see the entire church flourish. Many people in their sixties and beyond are vitally involved in both pastoral work and evangelism which, when combined with a strong parenting of the whole church, can prove to be a huge asset to the kingdom advancing.

The strongest temptations within the sixties are those that lead to a critical spirit that harks back to the good old days. The expression 'grumpy old men' did not come about by accident! Being involved in brand-new ministries can also keep the sixties-plus generation vibrant and fresh as well as full of new challenges and horizons.

Stage six can also be true for people who have left the sixties and are moving into their wisest years! Again, these life stages are not exact and many people exhibit some of the positive characteristics of a number of the stages outlined.

Creating a generational church is the clear way to creating a powerful twenty-first-century church that holds all of the strengths that each generation brings. It is our greatest challenge. Most new churches, however, can tend to be younger in age. This is generally a result of both the 16–25 window that gives the greatest evangelistic results out of all of the age profiles, as well as people's inability to transition to the next life stage the older they get. Life is long, and it's essential to growth not to just gain people quickly through the front door of church life while losing them quietly through the back door after they've completed just one of the six life stages that they were actually destined to complete.

The greatest challenge for each of us is to successfully navigate our next transition time between stages. If we do it well, we'll model it not just to those in their own transition between the same stages as us, but to everyone between every stage and in every transition. The results could be staggering.

10

The Myth of Destiny

God's Default Button

In my life as a pastor, I am around 95 per cent confident that God will do what he said he'd do. I'm not leaving 5 per cent for doubt but for the gazumpings of God. It appears that even though we like to think that things happened because we believed for them to happen, much of the direction of our lives is caused by default rather than design!

Reinhard Bonnke never designed his rise to become a huge evangelist in Africa. It came about through default as the advertised healing evangelist for a small crusade failed to attend, forcing Reinhard to step into his shoes. Through the powerful results of that crusade, Reinhard was catapulted into a new sphere of operation.

I once overheard my Assistant Director's reply when she was asked how she landed the job. Much to my horror at the time, she said that it was by default. She claimed that I had asked three other people before asking her. And that was the truth! Proverbs 16:9 'In his heart a man plans his course, but the LORD determines his steps.' It would appear that my attempt at offering the job to those other people of greater experience and age had been gazumped by God. I had planned the course – God had directed it!

It seems to me that our faith-life operates in two realms – the realm of what we see as the best outcome from our review of the situation, and our trust in a God who can see what we can't and knows what we don't. We believe as much as we can in the removal of mountains, the healing of bodies, the provision of finance and the removal of temptation. We believe that we will see answers to our prayers and faith declarations. Our ultimate destiny appears to be a mix of our believing in his promise, and the overriding providential hand of God.

Destiny is a complicated thing. Judas proved it! In sovereignty, he was the one who would deceive Jesus and fulfil prophecy. He was a marked man. In the daily grind of destiny, Jesus prayed for him and believed the best for his life, just like we do for everyone in our daily sphere of influence. Judas had the freedom of choice to not do what he did. Sovereignty looked back upon Judas's life and saw what he would freely choose.

The Recalculation of Destiny

For the simple purpose of looking at the workings of destiny, I want to leave sovereignty to one side for a minute. In a world where God respects people's ability and power to make their own choice, it appears to me that God is having to recalculate the details of destiny almost every nanosecond! This is especially true when someone fails to be faithful with the 'talent' they've been given. In Matthew 25, the master is seen taking away the 'talent' from the unfaithful servant and giving it to the most fruitful servant. The talent count began as 5, 2, 1. It then moved to 10, 4, 1 and finally became 11, 4, 0. It could have become 26, 0, 0 (2 times 11 plus 4) if the second man had failed to exercise any more than the tally of gifts he'd been given. This shows that you may be happily pursuing a defined destiny in God with the talents you've been given, only to find that you've been gazumped. You have now been given what actually belonged to someone else's destiny (again, putting sovereignty aside). You are now busier than you have ever been.

It Just so Happened

The most understated verse in the entire Bible is found in Ruth 2:3 which says, 'As it turned out, she found herself working in a field belonging to Boaz . . .' It just so happened! This was a collision of destiny that could only ever come about through the losing of one's life to gain it.

Ruth lost her identity to Naomi when she made Naomi's God her God, and Naomi's people her people. She also made Naomi's condition of poverty, her condition. She did her best, however, to relieve it. It just so happened that she was gleaning in her potential kinsman-redeemer's field, and it just so happened that she eventually became the great-grandmother of King David! Out of the ashes of sacrifice comes the phoenix of destiny. Not everyone chooses, however, to walk in the way of Ruth. The prize could possibly have been open to her sister-in-law Orpah, but she failed to rise up, and remained in Moab. Canaan could have been the inheritance of Terah but he stopped for good in Haran. It was Abraham, his son, who got it, but only through intense obedience and believing.

In the realm of destiny, we like to think that we're pretty much in control. It is that 'control' freakery that God loves to disturb. Just as James urged prideful people not to boast about tomorrow, God's ability to cut in on us any time he likes is like a shot across the bow of our ship of vision-making, goal-projecting and wise planning. God gazumps. Always has done. Always will.

PART 3:

SACRED COWS IN THE LEADER'S WORLD

Before I was saved I was both wicked and boring.
I thank God that I'm no longer wicked.

Anon

Introduction

There's a cult of success out there that somehow believes that failure has no part to play in the life of faith. I've tried to go from success to success, but with very little success! I'd love it, though – every seed planted bearing amazing fruit, and every project started leading to an avalanche of opportunities . . . I'm still hoping for it, yet it's this in-between stuff that I find really difficult!

There's a world out there that pigeonholes everything in degrees of success or failure. If you run a huge business or a huge church, you're deemed a success. If you run a small church or you're in a low-paid job, you're deemed to have either a small degree of success or some degree of failure. And it's this backdrop that causes even Christian leaders to lose one of the most vital ingredients of the Christian life – their *zing*.

In Part 3, we look at:

The Myth of You Shall Not Fail
The Myth of Summertime Christianity
The Myth of Holiness
The Myth of Praise
The Myth of Private Devotion

It's your opportunity as a leader – or emerging leader – to rise up out of your condemnation and hear the words that fell upon Jesus: 'This is my Son, whom I love; with him I am well pleased' (Matt. 3:17). It's time to get some more sacred cows in the middle of the cross hairs of our spiritual rifles!

11

The Myth of You Shall Not Fail

Failure Is Not an 'F' Word

Most Christians think that failure is a bad thing. I'm not so sure! If by faith we can order mountains to rocket off into the distance, why have there been whole mountain ranges that just haven't budged, even when we've been full of faith?

Some would say, 'Because of a lack of faith.' I would say that it's not always because of a *lack* of faith but often because of an *absence* of faith, which is something completely different. If faith comes by hearing from God, then it's possible that God never specifically said what we claimed he did. The transition of Scripture in the form of letter, poetry or history into an explosive bullet called a *rhema* word may never have occurred.

I now believe, however, that the overriding reason for the disparity between the 'certainty' of faith and the 'failure' of faith lies in our narrow interpretation of faith. We see it as an event – Jesus saw it as a journey. Almost every description he gave about the kingdom of heaven involved a journey (I personally prefer a 'shazam', but Jesus disappointingly never used this term.) 'A farmer went out to sow his seed' is all about the kingdom of God and that journey. It ends in the certainty that living by faith produces extraordinary results, but the riskiness and the failures of that journey are fully legitimized and accounted for in the parable (Mark 4:3–8). Failure is not final, nor is it to be avoided. Failure is not an option – it's a necessity.

Here are four truths about failure we all need to understand.

1. Failure is not an 'F' word

Jesus prophesied that not every seed scattered would produce a harvest. Some seed would fall on hard soil, some on shallow soil and some on overcrowded soil – all of which would not produce. The idea of 'perfect' faith-living is foreign to Jesus. The idea that the journey to success would be perfectly successful is not right – it has its seasons of lows and highs and eventually leads to something very high indeed. In the previous chapter in Mark's gospel, Jesus chose his twelve disciples. The maximum success Jesus had with the twelve was 92 per cent. Judas, despite the prayer cover the Saviour personally gave to him, failed. Why expect a 100 per cent success rate in the choosing of a ministry team or in the formation of a business when Jesus himself never achieved it? In fact, if you track forward a little, the success of Jesus' team proved almost disastrous from just before the cross to just after the resurrection. It depends when you cut in on the story. To date, the story of what eleven of the twelve disciples achieved, however, under the influence of the Spirit certainly proves the 30-, 60-, 100-fold increase that Jesus prophesied at the end of the parable.

'Mountain moving' may not be as instant as we interpret it to be. Our faith life may end up being a mountain-moving *story* rather than a mountain-moving *event*.

Most Christians, indeed most people, fear failure. We've created a perfectionist Christianity where the only reasons for imperfection are doubt and impurity. Outside of real faith, Christians have created a polarized environment oscillating between wanting to believe and not really believing. Faith and failure seem incongruous. Yet, through this parable of the sower, Jesus amazingly puts the two worlds together in the shape of a journey that started badly, yet finished brilliantly. Welcome to the faith life – and welcome to real faith – not just wishing to believe because of our wrong interpretation of failure.

2. Failure is the sign of future success

Seed scattered on hard paths is the sign that a farmer is in the vicinity. It's proof that someone with a sack full of seed is out and about somewhere in the field. Proverbs 14:4 says, 'Where there are no oxen, the manger is empty, but from the strength of an ox comes an abundant harvest.'

The presence of oxen may mean that the manger is a little messy and untidy, yet the outcome of the oxen is eventual success. The presence of ox dung indicates that success is imminent!

A number of years ago, we started a ministry called 'Megababe'. It was to be another ministry of the Megacentre in which we were already running Megakids and Meganursery. Megababe was to be a clothing agency where people from the inner city of Sheffield would give us their unwanted clothes to sell, and we would split the profit. The aim was to become part of the lives of local people and see an effective business established. All was not good from the start. Firstly, Matalan – a huge chain of department stores offering the cheapest of clothing – opened a store across the road. Secondly, one of the few takers of our great idea was a local transvestite who loved spending time trying on all of the clothes. Because of that, we lost the support of a number of our volunteers. Thirdly, Megababe, as the name suggests, was seen as either a store for babies' clothing or for very, very large women. After a short time, we cut our losses and closed its doors.

In itself, Megababe was a failure. But as part of a faith journey, Megababe was a sign that we'd set off on an adventure of making Jesus known to the local community. It was the evidence of desire, heart, pro-activity and entrepreneurialism. When the oxen of inspiration are in the stalls, the droppings of bad ideas and not-so-good ideas will litter the floor. The strength obtained from the great ideas and projects will one day far outweigh all that's gone before. From the ashes of Megababe, we have gone on to create Megalearn (teaching non English-speaking people language and computer skills), Megaconferencing and two other Megacentres. Our failure was a part of our road to success.

3. Failure is never final

The final instalment to every story of faith is incredible success. Hardship along the way may produce the internal success of character, and this then leads to great expectation (see Rom. 5:3–5) and great outcomes.

Faith does not disappoint. If God placed a word in your heart, it will come to pass – albeit not usually as the crow flies, but as a river runs! Generally, the words that God actually gives to us are non-specific – they relate much more to his nature and to a grand outcome than to a specific plan and detailed outcome. Because the logos of the Word of God is filled with the gazumping of the 'lesser will of God' with the 'greater will of God', we need to be open to the unusual, and to the invasion of the overriding and overarching will of the Father (that is also attached to our deeper desires and passions). When all is said, summed up and done, 30, 60 and 100 times that which is sown is the definitive outcome of good seed in good soil. And that is what all who live by faith are destined for, in both the ministry of this life and the magnificence of the next.

4. Failure is in the soil not the seed

In each of the soil conditions where the seed failed to bear fruit, the failure was to do with the environment, not the seed of the word. You may have failed, yet the seed of the word remains intact – it's just looking for the right environment to flourish. If you know that God has given you a promise, put your belief back in God and not in your history. You may have failed, but the future remains undaunted by it.

By failure and faith we enter into grace (Rom. 5:2). Grace is a gift from God. It originates from heaven itself. We did not create it. We need to separate grace from human effort. We can only effectively do this, however, in times of failure. These times prepare our hearts for our amazing season of success. Ego must be dealt with. Now is the time to see ourselves as successful traders of heaven – even in the midst of failure and disappointment.

It's also important not to over-fertilize the good soil. It is possible to start in faith and yet finish in the flesh (ask those Galatians!). Psalm 37 is the psalm which outlines what to do while waiting for a harvest. Because it's *his* harvest and not ours, it's important not to keep tinkering with the soil and pulling the seedlings out to see how they're doing.

There is an expression that is currently doing the world circuit which I think is incredibly detrimental to the journey of faith. It's the expression, 'If you keep doing the same thing, why expect different results?' In other words, 'If you've failed, it's time to try something completely new.' Faith, however, keeps on spilling and sowing the same seed and does actually expect different results. It expects that from the continued process of sowing we shall see an exponential return on all we do – eventually!

Failure is not something to shy away from – it's not an 'F' word – it's something to be enforced, expected and entered into knowing that it's never final. If your inspiration is from the Spirit of God you are on your way to an incredible future. The trapping of your failures are proof that the oxen of inspiration are in the stalls; you're on your way to a God-assured harvest.

The Myth of Summertime Christianity

12

Is 'Skint' a Lack of Faith?

When things are financially tight in church life, or even in our personal lives, it could be a sign that we're actually smack bang in the middle of God's will. Sometimes we just need a jolt. Our propensity for routine and familiarity slowly leads us away from noticing changes in season and changes in the mind of the Holy Spirit. When forced to really hear what the Spirit is saying we finally wake up and move out into new territory in God.

Being 'skint' is often a tool that God uses to re-educate both our individual lives and our churches. Sure, he wants us to prosper, but it needs to be accompanied by some changes that realign all we do and all we are involved in more directly with God's will for this moment in time.

To relieve your church or your home of financial difficulty, one of two things must happen – the income needs to increase or the expenditure needs to decrease. It's good to believe and pray for increased giving, but it is also good to forensically investigate whether the inner workings of your church or home are actually in line with the wisdom and blueprint of heaven. It takes faith for increase and faith for decrease. The difficulty with decrease, however, is that it often affects the people we love.

As leaders and emerging leaders, we have a 'pastor' and a 'coach' inside of us. In church life, upsetting the apple cart is not what the 'pastor' wants for anyone we love or work closely with. However, the 'coach' – who often takes a back seat through not wanting to hurt or destabilize anyone – is forced to take a more prominent role. Jesus Christ was both friend *and* coach. Coaching is a part of every true leader's role.

The decisions that we have made at Hope City under financial squeezes have proved themselves to be right decisions not based upon panic (even though we *always* panic initially!), but upon the underlying wisdom of God. There have been a number of different scenarios that have been brought to my attention during the lean seasons:

Scenario 1: People Who Have Drifted From the Heart of the Vision

Numbers 11 proves that behind every job in church life is a spirit of prophecy. When Moses' workload was eased and the Spirit taken from him and put on seventy elders, the elders didn't suddenly pick up their diaries. They all began to prophesy! Behind every job ought to be a heart beating in line with the vision of the church, which in turn is God's vision for the town/city and the region.

People naturally drift and their lack of visionary spark is only picked up in times of forced review. The core roles within a church need to be accomplished by people white-hot in love with the underlying vision. If the 'engine room' lacks power, the whole ship will slow.

Church staff who have cooled need a quick shot of power directly from heaven, or a reinvention brought about by a season of working outside the church. To reduce the budget through reducing or replacing these staff is not downsizing, it's right sizing – where the staffing of a church is revaluated in line with the current emphasis and movements of the Spirit.

Scenario 2: People Who Have Never Been Baptized into Church Life

I speak metaphorically and I concur with both being baptized into Jesus and baptism in the Holy Spirit. There is, however, a baptism that seems to take place from time to time for all those who wish to be in major leadership and positioning in the future of their church. There are rivers of sacrifice to cross that are greater for them than for some of their companions. Becoming a leader of many requires the greater sacrifice of being a servant of many. And the spirit of servanthood is periodically examined by the Holy Spirit. I have a number of young disciples who wish to change the world for Jesus. What they lack is the smell of a shepherd – the smell of someone who has experienced the ups and downs of humanity and desire above all to love it back to health. 'I have a dream' is great if you truly love the people you have a dream for. Expanding one's capacity to love is a key role of the Spirit.

Over the past twenty-five years, my church wage has been cut, non-existent, increased, severed, decreased, enhanced, capped, shunted and meddled with. Each time, it's challenged both my vision and my motivation. It's taken me back into 'faith land', and a little closer to the topsy-turvy world that so many I'm ministering to are a part of. It has taken me back to the reason I do it – to change a generation.

It's important not to shelter 'up and comers' too much from the front line of living by faith, and the lean times that are there to create a width and depth to their ministry. Changing wages and employment arrangements due to financial constraint can work a treat, but only for those who are envisioned to become a key part of the future leadership of the church.

Scenario 3: People Who Have Reached the End of Their Season

In the general workforce of the towns we live in, to stay in the same place longer than three years is miraculous! In church life we need to understand that very few roles are ever lifelong. To carry on a role for over five years is most unusual. Many of the roles in church life are seasonal. The one consistent thing is that we're all a part of the family, not all a part of the staffing. Some people should have left you six months ago but because we are creatures of habit, they're still there. Only through the prompting of financial constraint and the filtering of good financial investment are these people ever brought to account!

You can spot the tell-tale signs – inventing little projects while the existing projects are neglected; a little narkiness at times, revealing an inner unexplainable frustration; instead of concentrating on their own remit, snooping into other people's when they have no real business doing so; and a general disassociation from the corridor banter that is the social culture at the core of the church life. Sometimes when you try to find them, they're nowhere to be seen. And their mobile is switched off. How annoying! And what are they up to?

If you find you have to have time sheets for people who have not recently come on staff, they could be 'past their sell-by date'. It may be the end of their season.

Scenario 4: People Who Are Essential to the Future Vision of the Church

There are those staff members you can't move even through times of great financial constraint. There are those who have done their apprenticeship in previous seasons of lack and are not currently in need of change and reinvention. There are many who are vital to the organization's current health and there are still others who represent the key, new things that God is currently doing in the life of the church. They are all a part of the church's core strength and this season's tapestry of the Spirit. Sometimes a wage reduction can inadvertently sharpen the spirit of a good and vital 'worker', but it's important also that the reverse doesn't happen – a muzzling of the 'ox' while the grain is being trampled (see 1 Tim. 5:18). It's therefore essential that sensitivity is applied to every person's particular season and circumstance in order to effectively trim the sails without destabilizing the ship.

Every decision that we ever make needs to be on the platform of faith. It's faith, in fact, that often takes us into the lean times in order to prove its power and turn 'lean' into 'abundant'. A little financial squeeze can be good for a church (or one's family) as long as there is a commitment to personal capacity growth, a love for God and a desire to be a part of the future move of God. As a friend of mine once said, 'No one counts the cost of a shovel while digging for gold.'

If I were flushed with finance, I would hope that I would listen as closely to the voice of the Spirit as I do through the lean times.

Usually it's not the case.

13

The Myth of Holiness

Let Me Entertain You!

Entertainment has always been associated with either the superficial side of Christian living or the downright worldly side, but it has never been officially associated with serious Christian living. We all crave entertainment but alongside charisma, money and creativity, it's been sabotaged by the spirit of religion and left out in the cold to be snatched by the makers of *24* and *Lost*.

I'm on a mission to make church entertaining! It's a mission worth fighting for because 'boring' has seeped its way into the heart of church life with long-winded preaching, worn out songs, unrehearsed items and uninspiring leadership. We've accepted it as the norm, and lack of inspiration has been seen as par for the course. In reality, it comes down to compromised leadership, bad communication and lazy musicianship as well as an inverted resentment against all of the fun we've missed out on since becoming a Christian.

Bring back good old-fashioned entertainment I say! To entertain is to inspire, provoke interest, arrest and take people on a heart-lifting journey into the way, the truth and the life of Christ.

'Boring' is a state that should be banned forever in church life. Fair enough if it's a bored 15-year-old who has no intention of pressing forward in God, but if it's the inner third of your church, it's a different matter. In that case, whoever is leading the church and its services needs to be rebuked, retrained or retired!

Let's talk

Let's talk about communication. Truth alone is never enough to influence a generation, let alone 100 people on a Sunday. Revelation truth is better, but still not enough. Truth needs to be communicated in a way that opens the hearts and minds of the listeners. Without it, minds wander and ears are closed to the full potency of the living Word of God.

Communication is the bridge which spans the diversity of age, culture and maturity, and changes churches from being ineffective catapults that chuck things at people, to excellent distributors of pallets of wisdom and power.

Why do we accept teachers who can't teach, preachers who can't preach, and people devoid of inspiration? If they're 'on the curve' of learning, fair enough – but if it's because of a lack of ability to listen to the people they're trying to teach, there is something seriously wrong. Sometimes we allow 'boring' to continue simply out of respect for the person who's boring us. Respect is one thing that should not single-handedly dominate the landscape of our churches, creating untouchable people who have lost their elasticity for change and effectiveness. 'That's just the way they are' and 'Don't you know who it is?' are excuses that end up sounding the death knell for many churches and organizations. People end up voting with their feet. Even the great preachers of old such as Spurgeon and Wesley used all of their oratory skills to captivate and keep curious the crowds that gathered within the sound of their voice. The prime enemies of communication are:

1. **Lack of passion.** We don't want twenty-one points of information. We want to see a heart impassioned by the subject that's being taught.

2. Lack of portals. Each point needs an observational illustration or a personal illustration. Our services need that personal touch.

3. Lack of focus. We don't like long-winded and we don't like pet doctrines and phobias and philosophies. We want focus, not drivel.

4. Lack of humour. We want to swallow a truth and then have a little drink – *not* swallow, swallow, swallow.

5. Lack of sincerity. There is no such thing as a boring personality. Every person, whether they represent the rolling hills of Sweden or the Alps of Switzerland, are captivating to the human race. It's the lack of sincerity to their God-given personality that people can easily sniff out and then switch off to. People want and need authenticity.

Song Sung Blue

Ninety-nine per cent of songs we use in church services are disposable. Like a good razor blade, they're great for a season then simply need throwing away. An overused song is a blunt song, and a blunt song is an ineffective tool for worship. Why is it that so many churches insist on dragging out songs that took a minute to write, have lost their magic and no longer trigger a fresh response to God? Often laziness is the answer. A lazy church is a boring church, without edge, zip and spring to quicken the heartbeat of those who are a part of it.

It's time for new songs to roll off the production line – fresh, great lyrics, great new chord progressions and great new orchestration. It doesn't have to be rocket science – just doing the best with what's available.

How to Draw a Crowd

'Same old same old' is often the recipe for the day – same songs, same prayers, same announcements and the same people doing the same things. Variety is the spice of life. Being unpredictably unpredictable is the recipe for creativity. Creativity is a gift that needs to rise from the ashes of church life. I don't mean bring back Christian mime artists being trapped in boxes, or weird prophetic dance – just simple, intelligent, applicable creativity that produces freshness, sharpness and an immediacy that makes people sit up and listen.

Jesus said repeatedly, 'He who has an ear, let him hear what the Spirit says to churches' (see Rev. 2:7,11,17,29; 3:6,13,22). Our leadership must apply itself to that connection between the message, the messenger and the person. We've got to help people listen.

Here's a list of ten golden rules for pastors and leaders that are designed to ban 'boring' forever. They deal specifically with the issues of freshness, originality, creativity and gripping authenticity.

1. You must immediately stop faking it

You must be the same person in public as you are in private, and the other way round! No more changing your voice with an American twang upon entering the pulpit. I know it's tempting – but the best stuff comes from being the real you.

2. You must immediately stop 'doing karaoke'

Stop nicking other people's thoughts, scriptures, ideas and strategies – get your own (or at least give them time to become your own!). Get your own attitude, slant, agenda and revelation.

3. You must immediately stop being so limp

Stop being so nice, so accommodating, so accepting and so accessible! There's a lot of stuff in church life that just shouldn't be going on. Sure, we're called to think the best, but as leaders we're also called to protect the flock. It's time to reel in the vagrants and say 'no' to the super-spirituals amongst us. A bit of discernment wouldn't go astray.

4. You must immediately stop saying 'someday'

It's all 'yes' unless God says 'no'. What are you waiting for? It's time to put off procrastinating and make a start! Nothing is so difficult that you can't simplify and make the first step towards its completion. You don't need another feasibility study, community survey or fundraising venture. Just get started, and if you get wind of God's disapproval, then stop . . . but not until.

5. You must immediately stop doubting your call

Sure, we've all got a huge list of unfulfilled prophecies – some of which it is actually too late to fulfil. The truth, however, is that God's word has never come unstuck, never had an error in it and never been given without a forthcoming accomplishment. It is for us then to conclude that some prophecies have not come from God. Let's not get hung up on that. It was their sheer enthusiasm to bless you that made them slip into 'imagination mode'. Does it really matter? God's real word will be fulfilled – and there's enough of that to satisfy everyone. Don't lose faith! Get your zip back and stir up some of those creative juices for another fresh season in God.

6. You must immediately stop looking so nerdy

Why is it that so many in the 'ministry' neglect their health and general attire? It's time to get reinvented. Much of it comes from our interpretations of 'spirituality'. True spirituality, however, actually incorporates personal health and well-being. Often a fresh start in life is required not only internally but externally as well.

7. You must immediately say what needs to be said

There might be someone right now who is on your core team who is either dragging their feet, doubting the vision, acting independently or not in the right spirit. If you don't address it, it will get worse, not better. Get some courage and some faithful supporters and go for it; you've nothing to lose. There's nothing more dulling than leaders not leading.

8. You must immediately stop comparing yourself to others

It's not helpful. You are a frontier minister operating where no man or woman has gone before! If you've been called to break open the Wild West, why compare yourself to someone called to build on already populated fields? Who's the best – Timothy, Eunice or Lois? Answer: All are equal parts of the chain.

9. You must immediately stop being a conference junkie

Conferences are good, but too many are a waste. If you're like me, the temptation to imitate becomes too strong if we're always inundated with other voices. Leaders aren't just listeners or readers – they're thinkers. It's time to do some original thinking.

10. You must immediately stop being so serious

It's time to not be overly sincere, a little too worthy and excessively serious. You'll burn out! A sense of humour is God's release valve to help you overcome the emotional intensity of some pretty serious stuff. Maybe it's time to switch off Joyce Meyer and switch on Joe Pasquale! Some light relief will bring back the sparkle you might have been desperately lacking.

The best primary teachers are also the best entertainers. The best university lecturers are also the best entertainers. The best preachers are also the best entertainers. Jesus was thoroughly entertaining. He captured people's attention, created intrigue, drew crowds wherever he went, then went on to create disciples.

The one thing our church ministries lack is the one thing that Jesus was a master of – attracting the crowds. It's time to mix our life-giving, wisdom-enhanced, anointed ministries with a good dose of entertainment. There are boxes full of creative ideas that are waiting to be unlocked; ideas which will attract a whole new batch of listeners and learners. It's your prerogative to find those boxes and pour out their contents.

It's time to entertain.

14

The Myth of Praise

How to Have a Critical Eye

Before you criticize someone, you should walk a mile in their shoes. That way, when you criticize them, you're a mile away and you have their shoes.

Anon

Everyone needs a critic. I've done a lot of stuff that I have thought at the time was brilliant, only to return to it a few months later to realize it wasn't as brilliant as I thought it was. It's a human foible to believe too much in our personal ability to hold both detailed perspectives as well as broad perspectives accurately at the same time. Everyone needs a second pair of eyes!

Without perspective, it's easy to think you can sing when you can't, think you can't dance when you can, think you're fat when you're thin, and think you're thin when you're fat.

Now, don't pick on me for the following huge generalization, but I believe that a lot of our society's delusions and insecurities come from an absence of fatherhood. If there is a difference between the mandate of motherhood and the mandate of fatherhood, I believe it is this: motherhood says, 'You can do it' and 'Don't let anyone stop you or pull you down', and fatherhood says, '*This* is what you can do' and '*This* is what you were born to excel in'. Motherhood provides the river, fatherhood provides the banks. It's the river that provides the momentum and enthusiasm and it's the banks that provide constructive criticisms that are needed for great success.

Too much criticism, however, causes souls to shut down, minds to darken and spirits to shy away from anything that could involve more criticism. The paradox of those who flunk the *X Factor* is that it was often too much criticism of the wrong kind that actually drove them into the isolation that led them to a critic-free world of far-fetched imagination. In church life, heavy-handed criticism has also led many into a similar critic-free imaginary world of anointing, power and unlimited freedom.

It's time we learnt how to be *successful* critics, creating a culture of both encouragement and direction, of both river and banks. Here are six facts about criticism.

1. Criticism is specific, praise is general

Someone once said that we need at least one hundred words of praise to offset just one word of criticism. In my experience, it simply is not true. People have praised me 100 times and I have still been obsessed about that one statement of criticism that was thrown at me. The reason why praise is so limiting and criticism is so sharp is that praise is usually general, but criticism is usually specific.

In the past, people have left my church accusing it of a lack of real teaching. Since I'm the 'main teacher', it's actually been a personal attack on both my ministry and me. For the so many more who have enjoyed the teaching, I occasionally get a 'That was great today, Dave', or 'You preached brilliantly'. That's usually as far as it goes. The 'praise' or 'encouragement' says nothing about *why* it was good or *what* was so good. So, whilst the criticism spoke of a lack of depth, content and systematic outline, the praise spoke of 'good'.

In marriage seminars, they often speak about each partner's emotional bank account. You can only draw out what you put in. They say that if praise and encouragement adds one euro of emotion each time they're spoken, then one criticism can actually take out 500 euros in one withdrawal. It is, in fact, even more than that, as criticism is often remembered for life. The reason why we are so limited in our ability to correct and be positively critical is because our understanding of 'praise' has been marred by lazy generalizations and anaemic back-patting, adding little to the confidence of those who are recipients of it.

It's time to be praise specific – releasing hard-working praise that works out why something was good, and calls upon the power of words to communicate that 'why' in memorable prose. Only then can we participate in making it all so much better by being granted the access card to constructively criticize, aptly evaluate and courageously confront.

After a little training in my church, I have developed the beginning of what I hope is a 'cultural revolution'! People regularly email me after a service to specifically praise it, and the positive influence it's had on their life. All of my leaders know to not just tell me 'That was great' but why it was so great. And vice versa. I feel a health I've never known as I understand not only my failings but also my strengths and abilities! And that has opened me up to constructive criticism I would previously have been hardened to.

2. Criticism is often right words in the wrong season

In Genesis 1, God created lights in the sky to serve as 'signs to mark seasons and days and years'. I've recently been called 'ahead of my time'. I'm trying to correct that by doing things at the right time and in the right season. Freddie Laker built a 'no frills' airline that was ahead of its time. It collapsed – only to be replaced by easyJet and Ryanair whose success has come from being the right idea at the right time. 'Knowing the times' is everything, say the sons of Issachar (see 1 Chr. 12:32).

The problem with criticism is that, even though it may be completely true, it's generally delivered at the wrong time. People have said stuff about me that has been absolutely true, but absolutely wrong for the particular season it was heralded in. It's usually been delivered out of season through anger and resentment.

We only have the capacity to work on one or two faults at a time. Instead of picking on us incessantly about every sin and failing we possess, the Holy Spirit works to a logistical plan that discerns the correct criticism for the current season. That is the art of great leadership. It's the art of turning a blind eye to certain glaring issues, only to address them at a later date. In this way, we avoid being overly and destructively critical and avoid people feeling helplessly picked on. It preserves both morale and momentum.

3. Criticism is what makes us

James 1 tells us to 'Consider it pure joy' (v. 2) when we face various trials and tribulations because the product of these trials is both maturity and completeness. Criticism is what makes us become a bigger, stronger person. Persecution, which is a form of criticism, is what hits the fan only to become fertilizer to next year's crop of character and capacity.

When we first planted our church in Sheffield, we called it 'The Hope of Sheffield Christian Church'. Because our overt sense of destiny was easily misconstrued as elitism and the evidence of a rogue trader (in the cold light of day, I can't really blame them), we copped a lot of criticism and ostracizing from other church leaders. We also attracted a lot of elite Christians and more than our fair share of rogue traders to our meetings! Eventually, this led to a lot of internal criticisms and schisms. All of that has played a huge part in causing me to grow wider, deeper and further into God. It's created in me a confidence in God that has in turn created a strong and wholesome culture that is Hope City Church today (yes – the name did get changed!).

As both leaders and emerging leaders, we need to create a robust spirit where every word is turned around for the enlargement and inner development of the church. That's pro-activity at its highest level.

4. Criticism is the tool of a friend

Proverbs 27:6 says, 'The kisses of an enemy may be profuse, but faithful are the wounds of a friend.' An enemy holds back any criticism in order to seduce someone into a position of advantage. A friend tells it as it is.

If someone believes in my future and cares for my well-being, it's time for me to listen. If we've had a shepherd's heart created in us through loving our enemies and believing in the most straggly of sheep, then we've earned the right to speak into other people's lives. It's time to not baulk at the fear of rejection or the fear of people leaving us. It's time to exercise our right. If we can't correct someone without backlash, they're either not a sheep of our pasture, or so desperately insecure that it's revealed far deeper issues that need to be dealt with. An undisciplined church is an undiscipled church. An undiscipled church is a bankless river – flood waters that rise and fall with menace and carelessness. It's not what God had in mind when he spoke about his glorious church!

5. Criticism is a cure of the perfectionist

Many people have a perfectionist streak within them. They hate to be 78 per cent successful, or even 88 per cent. It's 100 per cent or failure. They say 'it's the winning that counts' not because of a pure will to win, but because of a fear of failing. It drives them into an unabated stress-filled world. Their self-criticism becomes self-destructive.

The way to help remove this curse is firstly, to realize the impossibility of perfection and try to accept it. Even an athlete has peak performance outings spliced with very average performances. 'Performance' has a cyclic element to it that we may not understand, yet needs to be embraced.

The second way to break the curse is to enlarge one's capacity to quickly put failure in the past and turn the page is essential for every 'perfectionist' to break the curse. Post-mortems are only helpful when held in an atmosphere of positive and not negative criticism. There is a time to let sleeping dogs lie.

I remember Andrew Evans, the former pastor of Paradise Community Church in Adelaide once saying simply to his youth pastor, during a difficult Sunday's service, 'Let's call it a day.' Let's draw a line and refuse to elongate the service, resurrect the service or do a post-mortem on the service. Let's leave it. It's the adjustment every perfectionist needs to make. The ability to leave it – to let the past be the past. A new day awaits.

6. Criticism is a two-way street

Matthew 7:2 says, 'For in the same way you judge others, you will be judged, and with the measure you use, it will be measured to you.'

It works two ways. Whatever level of criticism we give out we then invite on ourselves. If we're overly critical, we may find that the spotlight that this places back on us becomes too heavy a cross to bear. It's also important that we don't go round simply picking on others without a good look at our own personal habits. If there's a plank in our own eye, everyone will know about it and refuse to have their speck dealt with until our plank is removed.

A critical spirit is essential to create a critically successful church that impacts the world. That spirit needs to be impregnated by a praising spirit and it must know when to speak and when to turn a blind eye. The secrets of great leadership lie within our ability to enthuse and challenge, ignore and direct. Stand corrected!

15

The Myth of Private Devotion

Moving from Devotional to Devoted

I know a lot of committed Christians who just love their local church, yet they have a very poor devotional life. And I know a lot of Christians who have a regular devotional life, but are not committed to building the local church; their devotional time is devoted purely to personal infilling which never makes its way into the heart of the church.

What the church needs is more 'devoted' Christians – Christians who unite a strong and vibrant private world with a super-abounding public world that builds God a house. Either the Christian lives in a hugely busy church world that has no room for seven strong quiet times each week, or they live in a world of strong regular devotion but no real connection to the ebb and flow of church life. The solution usually given for this is for the pastor to preach a sermon on the power of prayer and relate it to every revival the world's ever seen, or to present a new daily Bible-reading and devotional prayer guide to be followed up by the small group leaders of the church. I have taken a different tack, which to many hardliners would appear a little compromised. I think it's brilliant!

The Food Analogy

I encourage my church to try to have around three home-cooked main meal devotions with God each week where they know that they've touched heaven, and they know that something of heaven has touched them – a place where the Word of God and their inner thoughts have been allowed to both collide and breathe, and a place to really intercede for the future. I also encourage them to have around two shorter 'takeaways' each week where the nutritional value may not be as strong, yet still contains a good source of energy. I also want them to enjoy quick and delicious spiritual 'snacks'. They're brilliant when there's no time for either a sit-down meal or to pick up a takeaway. Sometimes two to ten-minute prayer times amongst friends or colleagues can achieve mighty results.

The reason for such a relaxed approach to devotion is that if we put the bar too high, only those with OCD (obsessive-compulsive disorder), a perfectionist streak, or a religious spirit can keep up with it. The rest eventually stop altogether and become paralysed by their feelings of failure.

The One-Hour Challenge

The Garden of Gethsemane has become a template for devotions across the planet, with Jesus saying to his three tired disciples, 'Could you men not keep watch with me for one hour?' (Matt. 26:40). In the mid-eighties, the one-hour template was extremely popular with the help of the Lord's Prayer being divided into five or six modules to help attain the sixty-minute target. It certainly caught my attention, but I had to abandon it when my obsessive side made sixty a magic number – fifty-five minutes of prayer would never do! It's not healthy, however, to quote just one reference to an 'hour' and build a devotional movement upon it.

The Lord's Prayer is certainly a headline summary of the different facets of prayer, but there is no directive to refer to the whole of the prayer every day, and none to make it last one hour. King David prayed morning, noon and night, but the length and depth of his prayers were not individually recorded.

I believe that it's vital that we are vision-centred and not just time-centred when it comes to devotion. It's important to touch God and to hear from him. It's important to praise and declare, intercede and repent. Because life is seasonal and heaven has more to do with farming analogies than manufacturing analogies, all of these things take on a seasonal approach. Some weeks praise abounds, with prayer coming in second; other weeks, meditating on the Word abounds, with worship coming in a close second; and for other weeks, prayer abounds with reading the Word coming in a distant fourth! In this way, we connect with the ebb and flow of the Spirit, rather than the rigid routine of a programme.

I believe that the key for this century is to raise up 'devoted' Christians who combine a strong devotional life with a strong devotional heart towards the advancement of God's church and his people. It's time, however, to kill the cult of devotion and tailor-make a God walk that suits us and releases us to fire our particular sling with anointed accuracy.

My recommendation of three or so quality touches from heaven each week, as well as another two less intense connections, is a far better template than attempting seven sit-down fully prepared 'meals' each week. Devotionals then become accessible, sensible and highly purposeful. Their emphasis is not on time and they don't place people in the awkward predicament of having to have a huge spiritual meal every day. Many weeks the three strong encounters lead to more because the person wants this to happen, not because they're driven to it through thin Scripture references. Because of the nature of real life, both takeaways and snacks are readily available at God's 'counter' and have a very real benefit. If it's the way our outer life is sustained, then we need to model it in our inner lives. The principal goal, however, is that we give enough time to both humble our hearts in prayer and worship, as well as digest enough proteins, carbs, sugars, fats, vitamins and minerals in the Spirit that can sustain us for a life fully devoted to Jesus.

Devotional Versus Devoted

Acts 2:42 is the verse that provides the quantum leap into what 'devotion' is really about. 'They devoted themselves to the apostles' teaching and to the fellowship, to the breaking of bread and to prayer.' The chapter concludes with the results of this kind of devotion: 'And the Lord added to their number daily those who were being saved.' Here are the four big differences between the traditional evangelical devotional Christian, and the Early Church fully devoted Christian.

1. Devoted Christians build on proven truth

The Early Church devoted themselves to the apostles' doctrine – the full height, width and depth of it. Paul said to Timothy, 'The things you have heard me say in the presence of many witnesses entrust to reliable men' (2 Tim. 2:2). The apostles' doctrine stood for both the old boundary stones and the new. It stood for proven truth, not peripheral truth.

Often in 'quiet times' we're encouraged to get something 'new' every time from the Word of God or from the Spirit. Many who wait for the new winds of truth miss out on the real tenets of truth. Often in church life, we're looking to preach the new thing that will excite and ignite people to kingdom living. The truth is that most successful preaching (and most successful 'quiet times') is spent revising old words, not just listening for new ones. Most great churches build on the main platforms of truth – reinforcing them and reiterating them regularly. The *rhema* word is generally an old word that is expressed in a new way and from a fresh angle. Churches and Christians that hanker after new and hidden truths often miss the full topography and strength of the apostles' teaching. They replace wide with narrow, and mistake deep for shallow.

2. Devoted Christians believe in corporate success

The Early Church was devoted to fellowship. Fellowship differs markedly from friendship. Friendships are often mutual – two or more people feeding off each other for strength and support. Fellowship is far deeper. It unites people who would never have come together outside of their devoted living. Its basis is 'what I can give to others and what we can become together'. Devoted Christians see success in terms of all that, plus much more – the building of the fellowship of believers. Corporate success is their goal – a powerful church is the outcome. Traditional devotional Christians often see their 'quiet times' as a key to personal success only.

3. Devoted Christians build on the new covenant

The Early Church devoted themselves to the breaking of bread – the remembrance of Jesus' new covenant, through his blood. Devoted Christians wake up in victory as they recall Christ's victory. Devotional Christians often only feel victorious after the transaction of a 'quiet time'. Devoted Christians wake up on the positional reality of sins forgiven. Devotional Christians often only move into this reality through their time set aside with Jesus. It's essential that time is spent building a relationship with Christ, but never as a substitute for the bridge of relationship with God built through the cross, and the faith to put our confidence in it.

4. Devoted Christians have a lifestyle of prayer

The Early Church devoted themselves to prayer. Devoted Christians also set aside times to pray and intercede, yet the purpose is not to spend twenty minutes doing it but to reach the heavens and see awesome breakthrough. Devoted Christians lasso everything with prayer – the mountains, the valleys, the future, the present, the practical and the prevailing. Paul urged us to 'pray continually' (1 Thess. 5:17) which can only be achieved by being prayerful throughout the day, and not compartmentalizing the spiritual from the secular, prayer time from non-prayer time, the natural from the spiritual, and the devotional times from the non-devotional. Like seasoning, prayer is to be mixed into everything we do. (People who say, however, that they simply live in the spirit of prayer without setting aside a place and a time to pray usually end up doing neither.)

To build great churches, we need to move people from simple devotional living to powerful devoted living: 'And the Lord added to their number daily those who were being saved.' The results of both reuniting spiritual devotion with church advancement, as well as creating a sustainable yet powerful spirituality, can be mind-blowing. It's time for that quantum leap!

Epilogue

One could spend his or her life devoted to the assassination of sacred cows. The only problem with it is that that one could easily become just another defender of the faith, and lose out on being a hugely needed activist for the faith.

My purpose for writing this book and for shooting so many cows was to clear some more space for the healthy cows to abound and multiply. In amongst all of the dogmas and doctrines that I have isolated and taken aim at, I have made a clear decision to remain proactive and not reactive, a player and not a spectator and a goal scorer, not just a goalkeeper.

It's essential that each of us not only stand up for truth and justice, but never leave the field of play where lives are touched, souls are saved and our communities impacted by the love and power of the gospel of Christ. Let the church arise for such a time as this!

Endnotes

1   Sonia Orwell and Ian Angus, eds., *The Collected Essays, Journalism and Letters of George Orwell*, Volume 3 (New York: Hardcourt Brace Jovanovich, 1968), p. 6.

2   From a sign hanging in Albert Einstein's office at Princeton.

3   Charles Haddon Spurgeon, *Morning and Evening Daily Readings*, 23 April (Tain: Christian Focus Publications, 1994).

4   Alun Davies – Vice President of The Assemblies of God in Australia (Australian Christian Churches), quote from a lecture for S4 Network Summit 26 March 2008, Sunshine Coast, Queensland.

5   Lewis A. Drummond, *Spurgeon: Prince of Preachers*, Third Edition (Grand Rapids, MI: Kregel Publications, 1992).

6   Dave Gilpin, *Jesus, Save Me from Your Followers* (Bognor Regis: New Wine Press, 2006).

7   Simon D. McIntyre, *Simon Says* (Australia: Inspire Publishing, 2008).

jesus, save me from your followers

confessions of a confused leader

davegilpin